A TURKISH TRIANGLE

ANKARA, ISTANBUL, AND IZMIR

AT THE GATES OF

EUROPE

EDITED BY HASHIM SARKIS
WITH NEYRAN TURAN

THE AGA KHAN PROGRAM AT THE HARVARD UNIVERSITY GRADUATE SCHOOL OF DESIGN
CAMBRIDGE, MASSACHUSETTS

ISBN 978-0-935617-90-0

Book and cover design by Wilcox Design | www.wilcoxinc.com
Printed and bound by Kirkwood Printing, Wilmington, MA

CONTENTS

HASHIM SARKIS

PREFACE

Every classification of Turkish cities singles out three major urban centers while relegating the rest to the status of secondary cities. Istanbul, Ankara, and Izmir have been the major poles of growth and development in Turkey since the Republic was formed. Despite a strongly centralized system of planning and redistributive politics that favored agriculture and industrialization in rural areas and secondary cities, these three cities have maintained a rapid pace of growth and a polarity that has defied expectations and controls. The metropolis, the capital, and the port have also grown to organize the regions and secondary cities around them, to direct their growth and development, and sometimes to subsume them into their amorphous suburbs.

To be sure, these three cities have followed different paths in their modern history. From a fire that annihilated its business center, Izmir was rebuilt to become the port of the Anatolian countryside and one of the main links to Europe, especially during the postwar reconstruction period. Istanbul may have lost much of its imperial glory after the creation of the Republic and the transfer of the capital to Ankara, but it quickly regrouped under the administration of Adnan Menderes in the 1950s to reclaim its strategic centrality. From a population of about 1 million after World War II, it is now the biggest city in Europe. Modern Ankara was created as part of the effort to place the administration of the country near the center of the nation state, and yet it has moved from being an administrative center to an educational hub and regional pole in Anatolia.

Over the past twenty years, significant changes have occurred within Turkey and around it that have started to reshape the roles if not the primacy of these three urban poles. The weakening of the centralized planning system in Turkey in favor of strengthening local and regional authorities, the disintegration of the Soviet bloc and the rise of Turkic states as zones of extended Turkish influence outside Asia Minor, the increasingly volatile dynamics in the Middle East, and European promises and challenges have transformed the Turkish urban polarity in significant ways.

Through case studies focusing on urban history, development, and planning, the book examines the rise of these three main urban centers in Turkey and their roles in organizing Turkish territory. Through the study of the recent history of these cities by renowned urbanists who are involved directly in the planning of their respective cities, this book aims to answer the following questions:

1. How did these three cities, with different national roles and characters, emerge and adjust themselves to each other and to the nation state?
2. What recent regional changes affect this internal triangle, and how is the polarity reoriented toward other regions and centers outside the national territory?
3. To what extent have the differences between these three cities been shaped by national planning?
4. How have these differences manifested themselves in the architecture of these cities?

In addressing these questions, the three scholar-practitioners shed light not only on Turkish urban development but also on the conditions of cities in many developing countries. Ilhan Tekeli's introductory essay on urban historiography in Turkey allows for a reflective and comparative model that also advocates a more robust approach to Turkish urbanization and to the questions of charting the evasive urban condition in general.

ILHAN TEKELI

AN EXPLORATORY APPROACH TO URBAN HISTORIOGRAPHY THROUGH A NEW PARADIGM: THE CASE OF TURKEY

Urban planners are sensitive to the historical development of cities, but they do not typically dwell on the problems of urban historiography. Yet the narrative structured by the urban historian and the scenarios developed by the urban planner are based on the same logical process, termed "inference by reduction."[1] Therefore both processes face the same kind of methodological problems. In general, both sides fail to comprehend this association, because urban historiography is not scrutinized from the point of view of its positive contributions to urban planning. The failure of such critical evaluation limits the benefit of urban historiography to the performance of urban planners.

Two different approaches or paradigms exist in urban historiography today. One aims to describe the process of differentiation of urban space in time through socioeconomic processes. We can term this approach, brought to the field of urban sociology by the Chicago school, the "historical geographic paradigm." In this case, the historical approach is either considerered parenthetically or given a teleological character to support the claim of universal validity. In this paradigm, there is no role for a planner. Moreover, there is no place for individual preferences in the community.

The second paradigm involves interpreting urban history as the history of planning. Where there is no place for voluntary choices in the first paradigm, the second paradigm accepts urban history as a cumulation of such choices. In this case a powerful actor, almost deified, is seen as having immense powers of determination. According to accepted planning conventions, this actor can be considered as either the planner or the politician integrated with the planner. The history of the city is identified with the history of consecutive stages of planning. Yet the actual development of the city usually invalidates this hypothesis, as the historical development of plans does not correspond to the historical development of the city. More commonly, it becomes the story of plans that have not been implemented. These distortions stimulate a constant reconsideration of planning methodologies and the transformation of planning concepts. The negotiative and collaborative planning approaches of today include several other effective actors in the process besides the planner. As the predetermining role of planning decreases, the opportunity to identify the planning history of a city with its history of development increases.

The first paradigm is dominant in urban historiography, while the second is used more often in history written by urban planners. Here I will attempt to develop a third paradigm, because the first two paradigms fall short in explaining the urbanization experience of Turkey. The first paradigm assumes that the basic dynamic of society is the motivation of individuals to maximize their interests. The basic dynamic in the second paradigm consists of assumptions held by the planner or by society about how a "good" city should be. Therefore both paradigms are normative. These two paradigms leave out two determining factors of urban forms. The first is institutional structure, broadly defined. It includes the legitimacy frameworks of the buildings and related regulations that shape the city.

The second excluded factor is the lack of compatibility between the capacity of social actors and the demands of appropriated frames of legitimacy. Urban development in Turkey has been determined, to a large extent, by spontaneous solutions developed by society to remedy the incompatibility between frames of legitimacy and the capacity of actors. The third paradigm accepts this incompatibility as one of the basic dynamics that shape the city. So in this approach, urban historiography becomes embedded in society itself.

In the third paradigm, the inadequacy of social actors will be considered along with other types of inadequacies. For example, these inadequacies may be manifested as insufficient capital accumulation at the level of society, institutional inresponsiveness at the state or local administration levels, low capacity for plan making and control at the bureaucratic level, insufficiency of capital at the firm level, insufficiency of income among the middle classes, or insufficiency of income and skills among migrants from rural areas.

Ways of overcoming incompatibilities include a wide range of responses, including spontaneous and partially illegal forms of supply, bribery, the formation of mafia-like organizations, popular acceptance of the abuse of accepted legitimacy frames, creation of exceptions in space and time within the context of the accepted legitimate order, amnesties, and finally, the appearance of new regulations and arrangements. The implementation potential of these adjustment processes depend on political processes and the level of economic development. In countries such as Turkey, aiming to realize their adaptation processes within the context of a democratic regime, the kind of process adopted will be different from those adopted in dictatorships.

A mental experiment will show the superior aspects of this proposed third paradigm. Assume for the moment that we are to write the development history of the big cities of Turkey according to the second paradigm. In this case, the result will be a story of failure. This story will lead to accusations against those who have failed to conform with the plan or to demands for more authority, rather than leading to the preparation of more successful plans. The second paradigm, in short, condemns the planner to a negative evaluation. On the other hand, in the view of a history written according to the third paradigm, the planner will have obtained many means with which to increase the quality of his planning. He will be able to see clearly any compatibility between his aims (or the institutional framework he has accepted without question) and the capacity of society. He will have more realistic expectations, be able to devise new institutional regulations in conformity with these expectations, and be able to question institutional regulations that in effect push a section of the urban population to engage in illegal acts. He will also be able to develop proposals that enable different actors within different types of processes. An approach that accepts the superiority of this model of urban historiography will also have accepted the critical role of institutions in understanding urban realities.

THE DEVELOPMENT PROCESS OF TURKEY'S THREE LARGEST CITIES DURING THE REPUBLICAN PERIOD

I was asked to offer a comparative analysis of the development process of the three biggest cities of Turkey: Istanbul, Ankara, and Izmir. The new historiographic paradigm proposed here emphasizes not the differences in the urban development experiences within a nation-state but the similarities. In organizing the narrative of the three cities in accordance with the third paradigm, I will refer as well to the first and second paradigms, for contrast.

In the organization of this narrative, modernist legitimacy is to achieve central importance; therefore the narrative will follow the development of the modernity project in Turkey. In my previous work, I have analyzed the transformation of Turkey within the context of the modernity project as divided into four periods, a system that will be repeated here. The period extending from the second half of the nineteenth century to the proclamation of the Republic will be termed "shy modernity"; the 1923–50 period, "radical modernity"; the 1950–80 period, "populist modernity"; and the period from 1980 to the present, "erosion of modernity." This essay is to cover the narrative of development of the three cities since the establishment of the Republic; therefore only the last three periods will be addressed.

THE BUILDING OF A NATION-STATE AS A SOCIO-SPATIAL PROCESS IN THE "RADICAL MODERNITY" AND POPULIST MODERNITY PERIODS

World War I completed the disintegration of the Ottoman Empire into nation-states. The proclamation of a Turkish Republic involved both continuity and rupture from certain aspects of the past. The challenge was to derive a nation-state as a "radical modernity" project from a pre-industrial empire and create free citizens from imperial subjects. Although leaders of this movement had been raised in the "shy modernity" Ottoman project, deliverance lay in becoming a nation and in trust in science and technology.

Institutional reforms implemented by the leaders of the Republic were not undertaken according to a comprehensive theory. Yet as their work is evaluated today, it is possible to observe that they perceived the building of a nation as a socio-spatial process to a great extent. The spatial aspect of the nation-state building project may be defined by four components.

The first component is the proclamation of Ankara as the capital city. The founders of the Republic believed that a sense of national unity could not be developed within the cosmopolitan atmosphere of large harbor cities. After long years of war, the demographic structure of the country had changed, becoming become homogenized. With the building of the new capital city in the midst of this homogenized population, it was

expected that new standards and models of life of a national bourgeoisie would be created there. This lifestyle would serve as an example for the whole country. In other words, an identity was established between the success of Ankara and that of the new political regime.

The second component of the nation-state building strategy was the construction of a railroad system to provide for internal market integration. During the "shy modernity" period, railroad construction had been commissioned from foreign companies. These railroads connected agricultural hinterlands to harbor cities, thus opening the hinterlands to colonial powers. Such a railroad system resulted in the disintegration of the internal market instead of providing integration. The Republic administration was determined to implement an integrated railroad. The system was doubled in size and, more important, was converted from a tree-like scheme based on port cities to a network scheme, with Ankara as the hub.

The third component of the project was a government-sponsored industrialization program aimed at import substitution, which located factories in small towns along the railroad network. The fourth component of the nation-state building program involved public houses (*halkevleri*) located in most cities of the country. It was expected that the key features of the "radical modernity" project would penetrate the whole country from these focal points.

The modernity project of the Republic was comprehensive and indeed radical. Yet the nationwide transformation envisioned by the project failed because of the low level of development of the country, and especially the slow rate of capital accumulation. Nevertheless, implementation of this project prompted important changes in the relative standing of the three big cities of Turkey. The national economic policies of the

Republic that sought to build an internal market led to a loss in comparative importance of harbor cities such as Istanbul and Izmir, which lost population. When Ankara was made the capital city, Istanbul lost its administrative functions. Although Istanbul maintained its position as Turkey's largest city, Izmir failed to hold its secondary ranking. Ankara, growing rapidly, became the second-largest city. The impact of the "radical modernity" project of the Republic was reflected in the shaping of cities, after some delay. During the first years of the Republic, emphasis was given to solving the problems faced by cities, which had emerged from war within the institutional framework of the "shy modernity" period.

In the first half of the 1930s, new regulation such as the municipal law (Belediye Yasası), general sanitation law (Umumi Hıfzıssıhha Yasası), buildings and roads law (Yapı ve Yollar Yasası), and laws governing the engineering and architecture professions (Mühendislik, Mimarlık Meslek Yasaları) constituted the institutional setup of "radical

modernity" as related to urban development. These laws constituted a modernist framework of legitimacy for urban development, in which there was confidence in planning. Mere surveying skill was no longer considered adequate for the preparation of urban plans, and architect-planners were required to take on more responsibility. In this framework there was great emphasis on scientific knowledge as well. Therefore the legitimacy of building construction in any city now depended on a process conducted by architects and engineers. Traditional construction actors and processes were denied legitimacy. Priority was given to the realization of public sanitation in the planning and administration of a city. Municipalities now entrusted with far broader areas of responsibility compared to the "shy modernity" period were expected to modernize urban life. But these municipalities were to remain under the tutelage of the central government. In such a modernist legitimacy framework, urban development was closed to every kind of fait accompli and spontaneous development.

Today it is easy to conclude that this modernist legitimacy framework was incompatible with the capabilities of actors of the day. Yet it is also possible that conditions of that period made awareness of these incompatibilities rather difficult to acquire. The boundaries of this legitimacy framework were not clear due to the low rate of urbanization outside of Ankara. Depeasantization had not yet started in the rural areas. The rate of increase of urban populations was not high. Moreover, the populations of Istanbul and Izmir had diminished since 1914. Under these conditions land speculation did not exist, except on the outskirts of Ankara.

The Turkish economy was far from realizing the capital accumulation required by the accepted modernist framework of legitimization. Detection of this deficiency was impeded by the low rate of urbanization and by the Great Depression. Under the influence of the municipal socialist trend of the day, a large area of function was allocated to municipalities. With the fulfillment of these functions, it was believed, civilized urban life would be achieved. Yet sufficient income had to be allocated to municipalities. Due to an economic crisis, the municipal income law (Belediye Gelirleri Yasası) could not be passed. It was more convenient to attribute the failure to realize the level of investments required by the accepted legitimacy framework to the economic crisis rather than relate it to inadequate capital accumulation, which was a structural problem. In this case therefore it was not necessary to question the accepted framework of legitimization.

The most obvious example of the incompatibility between the accepted framework of legitimization and national capacity was the lack of trained planners. Turkey had been acquainted with practical urban planning in the "shy modernity" period, but this practice had largely consisted of an extension of surveying. Nevertheless, the "radical modernity" period had raised expectations for planning, based on the concept of the "efficient city." Those involved in practice in Turkey, however, did not have the necessary skills to meet these expectations.

Turkey attempted to close this gap by using different approaches simultaneously. International urban planning competitions were organized for large cities, attracting experienced, well-known planners to Turkey. This process started with the urban planning competition for Ankara, won by Hermann Jansen. The same process was repeated for Istanbul, but the final contract was signed not with the winner of the competition but with Henri Prost, who had completed the regional plan for Paris. While these planners were in Turkey, they were commissioned to prepare plans for other cities as well.

To prepare the city plans required by the municipal law despite the deficiency in skilled personnel, two central offices were established in Ankara. Preparation of the necessary plans with the limited number of urban planners available could be achieved only through centralization. These offices were the Municipal Development Council (Belediyeler İmar Heyeti), under the jurisdiction of the Ministry of Interior Affairs, and the Urban Planning Scientific Council (Şehircilik Fen Heyeti), under the jurisdiction of the Ministry of Public Works. Such a solution seemed sufficient within the planning context of the period. A third way of closing the gap was to invite esteemed planners fleeing Hitler's Germany to higher-education institutions in Turkey, to train architect-planners.

Although the modernist legitimacy framework accepted in the 1930s had not highlighted deficiencies in cities other than Ankara, evidence that this framework would be insufficient at a national scale was clearly observable in the case of Ankara. Ankara was growing at an annual rate of 6 percent. At this rate, the proposed legitimacy framework became inefficient. Land speculation had reached high levels, obstructing prompt implementation of prepared plans. For example, land values for the site allocated for a complex of ministry buildings, considered the heart of Jansen's plan, had risen so high that the government could not expropriate the land within budget limits. President Mustafa Kemal had to intervene, using his personal prestige and power. (The owners of the land belonged to his close circle of acquaintances. He made it clear that the government was going to expropriate the site within the limits of budgeted funds, and the landowners were not expected to object.)

The institutional framework that allowed for registration of a single building on a single parcel in a single name soon excluded middle-income groups from the housing supply. Ankara faced a continuing shortage of housing, which resulted in the appearance of barracks, the forerunners of squatter houses, and the development of exclusive housing cooperatives for government workers.

At the time it was not possible to interpret the phenomena as problems of modernist legitimacy, as we do today. Within the context of the single-party regime, when all eyes were on Ankara, interpretations focused on the weakness of central authority.

RAPID URBANIZATION AS THE "MODERNITY PROJECT" ASSUMES A POPULIST CHARACTER

Following World War II, Turkey embarked on a rapid urbanization process, as did other developing countries. The 6 percent annual rate of population growth experienced in Ankara in the previous decade was seen in all cities in this period. The first signs of the fact that Turkey's modernist legitimacy framework would remain inefficient in the face of such rapid urbanization had already appeared in Ankara. The multidimensional incompatibility of the accepted institutional setup with the capacities of the relevant actors in society became apparent.

One condition for control of rapid urbanization within the context of the modernist legitimacy framework is the provision of formal employment opportunities, housing, and infrastructure to the growing urban population. But provision of these elements depends on a high rate of capital accumulation, which did not exist. Yet this was not the only cause of the incompatibility between the accepted framework of legitimacy and existing conditions. The education and skills of migrants from rural areas were insufficient to sustain them in the city. The rapidly increasing population of cities increased land speculation, raising prices beyond the means of middle- income groups. This rapid increase in urban population also caused a rapid expansion of cities beyond municipal boundaries.

Mechanisms that may help eliminate the incompatibility between the accepted modernist legitimacy framework and the general characteristics of society, along with the inadequate capacities of social actors, are closely related to existing political regimes. During the early years of rapid urbanization, Turkey moved from a single-party regime to a multiparty democracy. This was a kind of democracy in which populist tendencies increased and patron-client relations became dominant. It is not correct, however, to attribute the type of compatibility mechanisms adopted only to the type of political regime. In this decade Turkey was also engaged in an industrialization program, and there was a need for cheap labor in the cities.

Turkey failed to develop a new legitimacy framework compatible with existing conditions, for several reasons. First, many countries experiencing similar difficulties also failed to develop new legitimacy channels. The core of modernist thought, aimed at achieving a single, universally valid solution, prevented the development of alternative legitimacy frameworks all over the world.

Second, the urban bourgeoisie (including professional planners) assimilated and defended the modernist legitimacy framework. In the face of rapid urbanization, these groups at first insisted on routing newcomers back to their villages. Yet as incoming migration reached levels where such measures would be absurd, they "imprisoned" the newcomers in the imaginary villages in their minds as "peasants in cities." It was expected that these migrants would learn to live within the modernist legitimacy models in time. This expectation, however, is contrary to premises of acculturation theory. These groups expected that in the case of two cultures coming face to face, one would be transformed into the other. Such an expectation may have removed the need to search for a new legitimization alternative.

When an attempt to identify alternatives is impeded, the solutions developed will seem to preserve modernist legitimacy, but a search for ways to overrule it will contin-

ue. In the case of urban development, modernist legitimacy required two conditions. First was the existence of a plan, prepared with scientific methods and announced to society, to direct the future of the city. The second involved applying scientific methods to each building (requiring formal permits for starting construction and for opening to residents). This framework of legitimacy was supposed to exclude every kind of fait accompli. Yet in reality, although this legitimacy structure was seemingly upheld, it was being undermined by spontaneous and unexpected developments.

Some examples from housing, mass transportation, and planning practice show how the framework of legitimacy was undermined by spontaneous developments and how these developments were presented as implementations of the modernist legitimacy framework. The first serious impact of rapid urbanization was the housing shortage. Spontaneous solutions developed to overcome this problem involved new ways to supply housing.

The populations most constrained by the demands of the modernist framework of legitimacy were the multitudes that had left rural areas for cities. Government regulations did not give them a chance to sustain their lives in cities without becoming outlaws, and soon the cities were encircled by *gecekondu* zones, or squatter settlements. Although the populist democratic regime did not attempt to develop new legitimacy frameworks, it was nonetheles tolerant of this phenomenon, compared to the approach of dictatorships. Thus the *gecekondu* neighborhoods of Turkey have always been superior in quality and appearance to their Latin American counterparts.

Governments kept trying to reconcile the existence of *gecekondus* with the framework of modernist legitimacy. The solution developed was the passage of successive amnesty laws. With these laws, unauthorized settlements were pardoned in certain areas and for certain periods of time, outside of which modernist legitimacy sustained its rule. Yet the building of new *gecekondus* went on. In time, the *gecekondu* building process became partly integrated with market processes and partly with mafia-type organizations, and finally it became impossible for newcomers to build *gecekondus*. Radical political groups then provided *gecekondus* in exchange for political loyalty. So the forms of support of the *gecekondu* stock reached a high level of complexity.

The second spontaneous housing solution was "build-and-sell" (*yapsatçı*) housing. The house-building potential of the middle classes, for whom this solution was appropriate, was far higher than that of newcomers to the city. The middle classes faced a housing shortage when rapidly rising land prices eliminated the practice of registration of a single building on a single parcel of land in a single name. The build-and-sell solution enabled the middle classes to share the cost of a single parcel of land through fragmentation of ownership. This solution appeared when small developers started

acquiring land—the development value of which had increased in older parts of cities—from landowners in exchange for a number of apartments in multistory housing they built. The rest of the apartment units were presented to the market.

This, too, was a spontaneous development, but it led to formation of residential areas with densities far higher than those foreseen in plans and with inadequate infrastructure. It was easier for governments to present this development as congruent with modernist legitimacy models, compared to *gecekondus*. The government put forward a law allowing for the registration of a building in more than one name, including rules organizing the management of apartment buildings. With new development plans increasing the number of stories in the three big cities, building densities were increased, so the build-and-sell type of housing seemingly remained consonant with modernist legitimacy models.

Another spontaneous development was the introduction of the *dolmuş* (shared vehicle) transportation solution. Before World War II, inner-city transportation demand was met by public transport. After the war, in the face of the rapid increase in urban population and its uncontrolled expansion in space, municipalities failed to provide a concomitant increase in the supply of public transportation. This gap was filled by the development of the *dolmuş*—that is, service supplied by small entrepreneurs. Old taxis were modified to carry more passengers, who shared fares, reducing the cost to levels affordable to middle- and low-income riders. The gap in public service was closed by provision by the private sector, and thus local administrations could not hinder development of the *dolmuş* system given that their own supply of service was inadequate. Their contribution was limited to organizing the dolmus system along particular lines in the city.

The influence of such spontaneous measures and of efforts to sustain at least the appearance of modernist legitimacy models resulted in the three largest cities displaying a similar growth pattern: expansion of the city along intercity highways, high-density inner-city development, and growth of the central business district toward high-income neighborhoods. In this model of growth, provision of social services in the high-density city center remained inadequate, green areas were taken over by development, traffic congestion was worsening, and cities were losing their identities as old urban fabric was replaced by build-and-sell apartment blocs. *Gecekondu* zones were also encircling these cities. The population of the three big cities increased greatly, making Istanbul, Ankara, and Izmir metropolitan cities. But cities that grow in this way do not possess the structural characteristics of metropolises of industrial economies; it is perhaps more appropriate to call them overgrown industrial cities.

It may be expected that in this situation, regimes aiming to sustain the modernist legitimization framework may have attempted to develop new planning approaches. Planning was always defended as the legitimate solution in political statements of the day. Yet there was never any attempt to provide for a planning organization equipped with a trained workforce and the authority and knowledge necessary for successful planning, and channels of spontaneous developments have been left open—an approach that may be seen as hypocritical.

One challenge to the legitimacy of planning was through the increasing implementation of local partial development plans. At the time, major developers with significant capital accumulation had not yet appeared. Development rights covering large areas were therefore created through numerous local plans prepared by real estate firms, which also organized land speculation. These partial development plans functioned as a fait accompli mechanism, undermining urban development plans (although they too were called "plans").

Those who used local partial development plans to undermine the legitimacy of planning were small-scale capital owners who could also make use of political channels within the context of populism. In this period, another means of undermining urban plans was developed by the most powerful political actors. In Turkey this practice has been called "development operations." The unregulated expansion generated by these operations was sometimes tied to political figures seeking prestige (e.g., the work sponsored by Prime Minister Adnan Menderes). In these operations, priority was given to solving the daily problems of the people, while sidestepping planning oversight. At times, even the rules of law were bypassed.

Istanbul was the exclusive location of large development operations. The Menderes operation of 1956–60 and the Bosphorus Bridge and beltways project of Prime Minister Süleyman Demirel in 1967–73 may be mentioned in this context. The other two major cities were not subjected to these developments. In Istanbul, these operations could not be sustained for long periods of time, but were typically abandoned within four or five years, given growing resistance within professional circles.

The "populist modernity" period witnessed the establishment of the Ministry of Construction and Resettlement (İmar ve İskan Bakanlığı), which functioned like a ministry of urbanization; the institutionalization of urban planning education; the requirement by the Provincial Bank of the existence of city plans as a condition for the provision of infrastructure to cities; and finally, the establishment of metropolitan planning offices in the three big cities. These developments may be cited as steps taken toward planned legitimacy. The passage of laws to protect historic urban fabric from demolition should be added to the list.

Urban development in Turkey thus proceeded partly through plans and partly without planning, creating a unique development dynamic. Yet this practice is quite consistent with the populist and clientalist structure of Turkish politics.

THE EROSION OF MODERNITY IN A GLOBAL WORLD

Nineteen-eighty was an important landmark in Turkish history. A process of industrialization through import substitution (that is, an endogenous development policy based on internal development potential) was followed until then. From 1980 on, a new and open development policy based on exports was tried. As state entrepreneurship waned, priority was given to the private sector. This transformation brought about a radical change in how Turkey established relations with the rest of the world. About ten years later, disintegration of the socialist block and the end of the Cold War also provided important opportunities for Turkey to open its economy.

Most important of all was the worldwide transformation brought about by the 1970 economic crisis. The transition from industrial society to knowledge society, from the Fordist type of production organization to a flexible type, from the world of nation-states to a globalized world, and from modernist thought to postmodernist thought constituted the main dimentions of this transformation.

Turkey's attempt to adapt to this new world by transforming its external relations was reflected in important changes in its settlement patterns. In the "radical" and "populist modernity" periods, Turkey had achieved integration of the internal market. As Turkey opened its economy to world markets and integrated with global systems, important changes started to take place in the distribution of population. Population concentration occurred in the southern and western coastal cities, and Istanbul also began to grow rapidly. Istanbul started to regain functions that it had lost in the 1920s after the Soviet and Turkish revolutions, which would give it the status of a global city. While Istanbul was taking its place among the megacities of the world, urban planning circles in Turkey preferred to apply the concept of "world city" to describe it.

After 1980, not only the external relations of cities but processes determining their structuring and expansion also changed. Cities that had grown through the addition of individual buildings, based on individual decisions, or through the decisions of small-scale developers, now grew through organizations that brought together a large number of individuals or through large additions to urban space by powerful actors. Cities could now grow by the addition of large built-up areas through institutional arrangements, leading to new building-supply methods. The most important of these is mass housing deriving from the build-and-sell method.

Mass building was not reserved for residential areas but was applied to business needs as well, including organized industrial zones, warehouse sites, wholesale trade centers, transport services sites, specialized production sites, free trade zones, and the like. In all these examples, small-scale developers or even individuals were organized in cooperatives or other institutional forms to realize large-scale operations.

With cities growing through the addition of large fragments, central business districts started to experience a loss of function. The most prominent example was seen in Istanbul, where the old city centers of Eminönü and Beyoğlu could not meet the new control and management requirements. New functions adopted by the city created a new central business district of skyscrapers along the Mecidiyeköy and Maslak axes. This development has been closely related to the capacity of the system to mobilize large amounts of capital for construction.

For this period it is no longer possible to describe the development of the city with reference only to the pattern of expansion to new areas. Although the city continued to expand, important transformations were taking place in the old urban zones as

well. These transformations were numerous and most prominent in Istanbul. In this city, three factors were responsible for determining the kind of transformation that was occurring.

The first factor is new development dynamics that transformed Istanbul and, to a slightly lesser extent, Ankara and Izmir, from overgrown industrial cities to city-regions. This tranformation prompted important functional changes, especially in the city center. For example, although Eminönü lost several of its production and service functions, it gained important touristic and cultural roles. A similar process has taken place in Beyoğlu.

The second change is in the transport infrastructure and supply of service. In this period, all three cities borrowed large amounts of capital to realize public transportation projects. Congruency of the first and second factors opened the way to gentrification in some neighborhoods near the city center, as in the cases of Cihangir and Kuzguncuk.

The third factor is environmental. The risks from older *gecekondu* and other substandard building stock eventually reached an intolerable level. Istanbul's earthquake increased pressures to address the poorly made building supply. It remains to be seen whether this transformation will take place through large-scale municipal projects, as in the Dikmen Valley project in Ankara, or through build-and-sell processes based on development and improvement plans *(imar ıslah planları).*

But what about modernist legitimacy in these cities that are expanding in space while experiencing transformation of their central districts? Unauthorized construction is no longer specific to the *gecekondu* housing stock. The number of unauthorized buildings has risen, even in high-income quarters of Istanbul. Instead of *gecekondus* moving within the framework of modernist legitimacy models over time, other building projects have come to operate in the mode of the *gecekondu* builders.

These developments result when a city grows through the addition of large built-up areas. It is possible to control city growth, to a certain extent, through planning if growth occurs by marginal additions. In a city where large segments are added to the existing macro form, however, the actors manipulating this type of development are powerful—so powerful that they do not mind paying the high costs involved. They will use their power to materialize the type of projects they want on the land they have bought. Thus a fait accompli is created the moment a large parcel of land is bought.

In developed democracies, it is no longer possible to control urban development using plans of the old type, which represent a city frozen in time. Today urban development is directed by strategic plans prepared through public participation, and open to deliberative processes, to benefit from emerging new opportunities. Implementation of plans in Turkey, however, should not be confused with the transparent deliberative processes of developed democracies. Practice in Turkey involves mayors using their

authority in a nontransparent way, fueling rumors of the misuse of this discretion. Meanwhile, the demands of civic groups for increased municipal authority in the name of national decentralization and participatory democracy have been used by mayors to increase their discretionary powers even further. City administrations have not been democratized completely yet, and strong municipal authority has created local fiefdoms rather than widespread participation in most cases.

CONCLUSION

I have come to the end of the story, covering eighty years of development of the three big cities of Turkey—a story of modernization, democratization, and urbanization. It is a process of urbanization that has been completed in a far shorter time and with inefficient capital accumulation, as compared to European cases. The urbanization process of Turkey has taken place during the lifespan of a human being. Evaluation of this experience using modernist legitimacy models will lead to negative appraisals. If the Turkish experience is evaluated outside standard models, however, there is much to learn from it.

Comparative studies are necessary for a better understanding of the value of the Turkish experience. If these studies are conducted according to the first and second historiographic paradigms, there can be nothing beyond a predictably generic conclusion. But if this comparison is performed according to the approach proposed here, it will be possible to understand the development of cities as it has occurred in their own local situations.

Note
1. "Reductive inference" is a term used in logic to distinguish the reasoning of the natural sciences from that of history. In science, effects are inferred from causes; in history, however, causes are inferred from effects.

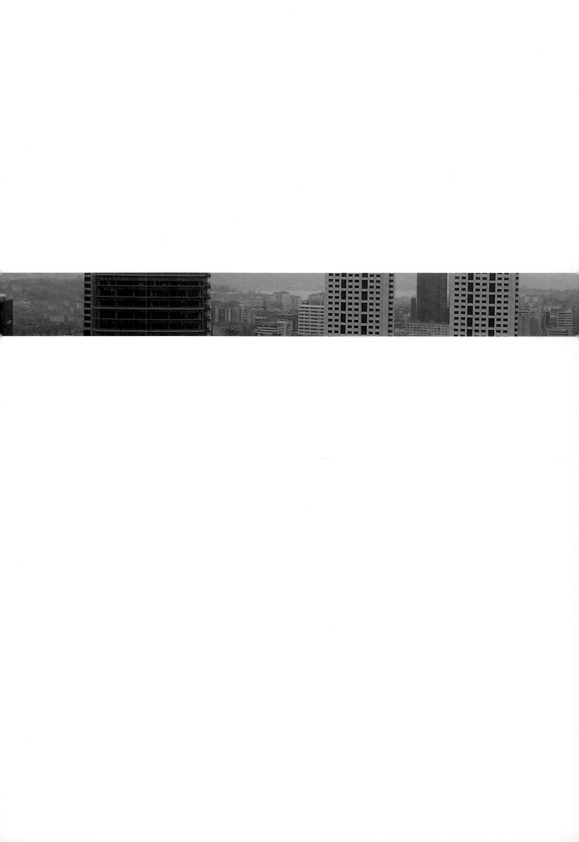

ZEYNEP MEREY ENLİL
AND HÜSEYIN KAPTAN

ISTANBUL:

GLOBAL ASPIRATIONS AND SOCIO-SPATIAL RESTRUCTURING IN AN ERA OF NEW INTERNATIONALISM

Istanbul is the most prominent city of what has been called in this volume the Turkish Triangle. As the imperial capital of two great civilizations, Byzantine and Ottoman, Istanbul has a different historical trajectory from the other leading cities. For hundreds of years it enjoyed a privileged status as the seat of political and economic power, until its prominence was challenged in the last century. Internationalization of the world economy, however, presents new possibilities for Istanbul to assume a more significant role.

Since the early 1970s, restructuring of the world economy has been characterized by deregulation, privatization, the opening of national economies to international capital, and the increased participation of national economic actors in global markets. This restructuring has been facilitated by technological innovations in communications and transport; other major indicators have been the emergence of a new geography of production marked by the dispersal of manufacturing activities around the globe and a concomitant growth of finance and other highly specialized services (Sassen 1991, 2002). Another key feature of this process has been the concentration of activities such as legal and accounting services, management consulting, and financial services in a number of centers, leading to the emergence of a new international hierarchy of cities (Sassen 1995, Blakely 1992, Friedmann 1986). Cities such as New York, London, and Tokyo are the major command-and-control centers in this emergent landscape, while a host of second- and third-tier cities play an important role in the global network as supranational and supraregional nodes (Sassen 2002, Beaverstock 1999).[1]

In this emergent hierarchy, there is harsh competition among cities to attract investments, trade, tourists, and skilled labor, and to be centers of finance, culture, creativity and innovation, and tourism. Attempts at reimagining and recreating urban space to this end have been manifested in large-scale yet piecemeal projects (Swyngedouw et al. 2002, T. Hall 1998) in the advanced cities of the West as well as those of the developing world including São Paulo, Buenos Aires, Bangkok, Taipei, and Mexico City (Sassen 1995). These included state-of-the-art office buildings in city centers, luxuri-

Istanbul as a nodal point in the global context.

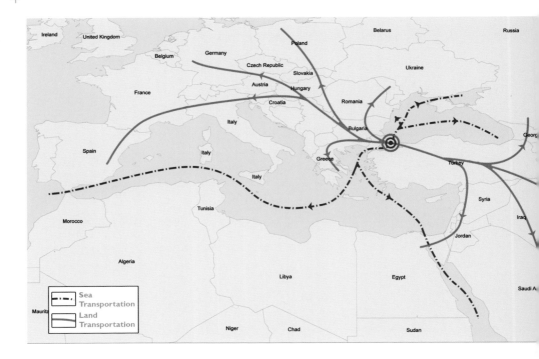

ous hotels and restaurants, convention centers, shopping centers, museums, upscale boutiques, wine bars, cafés, and luxury housing.

Another characteristic of cities striving to integrate with world markets, albeit with varying degrees of success, has been sharply polarizing income distribution. This has been seen in the creation of high-income urban elites, whose lifestyles do not change much from one place to another, as well as increasing poverty, leading to the emergence of a new underclass.[2] The resultant social exclusion and marginalization that create "seas of despair" (T. Hall 1998, p. 97) in the midst of affluence, abundance, and pleasure have come to mark the social conditions in cities under the influence of globalization (Swyngedouw et al. 2002, T. Hall 1998).

Emergent global trends and the restructuring of the world economy, which has moved toward integration with unprecedented speed and intensity since the 1970s, eventually impelled Turkey to adopt liberal economic policies and open its economy to international capital and commodity flows. In the new era of competition among cities, Istanbul has been the stronghold of Turkey's intensified integration with the world economy since the 1980s. Indeed, it was mainly through Istanbul that the project of integrating the Turkish economy with global markets was to be achieved. Reinforcing the attempts to redefine Istanbul's status were political shifts in the region, including the dissolution of the Soviet bloc, the rise of the Turkic states following the collapse of the USSR, and new dynamics in the Middle East. These changes created opportunities for Istanbul, as no other major centers could vie with Istanbul in a vast area that stretches from the Balkans to the Middle East.

To be sure, Istanbul is no longer the administrative center of the Turkish state. Nevertheless, the city is the most prominent economic as well as cultural node of the country. In this chapter, we trace this project of integration with the world economy through Istanbul. We first give a brief history of the development of the city since the nineteenth century, to contextualize these policies before discussing their ramifications for the socio-spatial formation of the city.

FROM A FLOURISHING METROPOLIS TO A SHRINKING CITY (1800–1950)

The integration of Istanbul with the capitalist world economy is not new but has its roots in the nineteenth century, an intense period of sociopolitical, economic, and cultural transformation in Ottoman society. Gradual secularization, a move toward centralization of political power, and the creation of a legal system outside the Şeriat were the main themes of nineteenth-century reforms. In the economic sphere, the 1838 Anglo-Turkish Commercial Treaty, the first in a series of agreements made with European nations, marked a new phase in which Ottoman markets were integrated with the expanding economies of the industrializing West. These agreements granted privileges to European traders and profoundly increased the volume of foreign trade. Istanbul was attractive to traders looking to benefit from these treaties and thus became a node in European networks of commerce. Nineteenth-century reforms and new economic

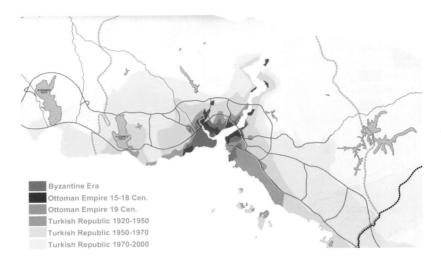

Historical development stages of Istanbul.

Nineteenth-century apartment buildings in Pera along the Grand Rue de Pera (today's Istiklal Street). Photo: Serkan Sınmaz.

relations had important effects on the cultural system as well. The classical Ottoman social system was altered by the emergence of a new Muslim bureaucratic elite and a non-Muslim commercial bourgeoisie who were agents of social change.

Opening the empire to foreign trade and investment required new institutions. Banks, insurance companies, and trading firms began to emerge in the city with concomitant office building types, which concentrated in Galata, turning the district into an international center of trade. Thus the prestigious commercial center of the city was no longer the *bedesten* and its vicinity located in the old city of Istanbul, but Galata.[3]

In parallel with economic expansion, Istanbul experienced rapid population growth: from 359,089 in 1829 (Karpat 1985, p. 103) to 873,575 by 1885 (Shaw 1976, p. 266). This surge forced the city out of its early nineteenth-century boundaries. The tides of change favored a particular pattern of growth; the city grew toward the north, leading to the rise of Galata and Pera on the northern banks of the Golden Horn.

Pera became a boom town and developed as a prestigious residential area. The emergent commercial bourgeoisie, predominated by non-Muslim merchants, bankers, and middlemen who prospered with the increased volume of trade, began to move their residences from the old city to Pera, near their workplaces in Galata. Another factor that encouraged the development of the city toward the north was the transfer of the imperial residence from the Topkapı Palace in the old city to the newly constructed Dolmabahçe Palace on the shores of the Bosphorus, then to Yildiz Palace in the hills of Beşiktaş. The Muslim ruling elite followed the Sultan and began to move to new residential areas close to the imperial residence. The old city was increasingly left to people of modest means.

New economic relations brought the penetration of Western lifestyles, resulting in altered patterns of consumption and the emergence of new institutions and enterprises. Hotels, theaters, glittering shops, and social clubs were concentrated in Pera in the service of the emergent bourgeoisie and the Muslim ruling elite, who had acquired international tastes. Luxurious restaurants, European-style cafés and nightclubs emerged in the city in an effort to emulate European urban life, making Pera the cultural hub of the developing metropolis (Çelik 1986).

The collapse of the Ottoman Empire in the aftermath of World War I and the inauguration of the Turkish Republic in 1923 marked the beginning of a new era for Istanbul. With the declaration of Ankara as the administrative center of the new state, Istanbul lost its status as capital city, which it had enjoyed for centuries. At the same time, changing contours of the postwar world economy led Istanbul to lose its network of commercial relations and thus its standing as an important port city and a vibrant center of international trade.

As a result of these political and economic developments, Istanbul lost almost half of its population, which was around 1.1 million in 1897. By 1927, it amounted to only 690,857 (Tekeli 1992, p. 21). In addition to wartime losses, two other factors accounted for the decrease. First, government bureaucrats left for Ankara. Second, the city lost the majority of non-Muslims.[4] Losing these two groups exacerbated the city's economic problems; non-Muslims dominated Ottoman foreign trade through strong ties with Europe. They and the bureaucratic cadres were vital for the economy of Istanbul because they were also the major investors in the city, and with their high incomes, they comprised a major market for consumer goods.[5]

After World War I and the Turkish Independence War, there was an urgent need to address the devastation, yet the building program of the early Republican years gave priority to reconstructing war-stricken Anatolian towns, developing the new capital, Ankara, and building bridges and railroads to connect and consolidate the country. Regenerating the economy of Istanbul and rebuilding neighborhoods that had been devastated by fire was not a priority.

It was at this recovery stage that the young republic was hard hit by the Great Depression. The liberal policies of the early 1920s were replaced by etatist policies in the 1930s and 1940s, geared toward nurturing industries deemed essential for economic development; there was not yet a fully fledged capitalistic class whose accumulation was adequate to invest in these areas (Lewis 1969, pp. 286–287). The building program of the early Republican years was further developed during the 1930s and 1940s. Scarce resources were again allocated to developing Ankara, establishing industry and service facilities, building model schools throughout the country, and constructing public works in the main cities and towns (Batur 1984, pp. 68–69).

Istanbul did not benefit from the etatist policies, as industrialization efforts and building programs largely targeted the inner parts of the country. The Ottoman Empire lacked a truly developed industrial base, and its capital, Istanbul, was far from an industrial city. Although the improvement and nationalization of existing industries during this period helped to alleviate the problems of a shrinking economy, the question of what would be a viable economic base for the city would occupy the administrators of Istanbul for some time (Tekeli 1992).

THE URBAN STRUCTURE AND EFFORTS TO REMEDY THE PROBLEMS OF THE SHRINKING CITY

In the shrinking city of the early Republican era, all neighborhoods and districts faced population loss. Desolation marked various parts of the city, especially those devastated by fires. The only exceptions were Pera or today's Beyoğlu on the northern banks of the Golden Horn and the newly developing neighborhoods further to the north, Şişli, Nişantaşı, and Teşvikiye, which continued to enjoy a privileged status.

From the Bosphorus to the coasts of the Marmara Sea, Istanbul stretched over a vast area on the European and Anatolian sides of the city. As the transportation network was improved by the introduction of tramlines, steamboats, and railroads during the second half of the nineteenth century, the city expanded along the newly installed infrastructure. Steamboats operating on the Bosphorus facilitated the growth of villages and turned seasonal houses into year-round residences. Similarly, the railroads connecting Istanbul to Europe and to the Anatolian hinterland also served as suburban lines, triggering the formation of summer resorts as well as railroad suburbs along the coasts of the Marmara Sea. As a result of this pattern of growth, the macro form of the city was extremely disproportionate to its population, which made the provision of municipal services difficult and costly (Tekeli 1992).

Planning efforts sought to remedy this situation. The most significant was the master plan by French planner Henri Prost. The Prost Plan, approved in 1939, envisaged a compact city form for Istanbul and gave priority to vehicular traffic. It proposed the opening of new roads and the enlargement of existing ones to condense the city that stretched over a disproportionately large area along tram and ferry lines as well as railways. It was expected that the integration of the scattered parts of the city would facilitate the renewal of the desolate areas, especially within the Istanbul peninsula.[6]

The Prost Plan was mainly concerned with the physical layout of the city and did not include provisions to address economic stagnation. Istanbul would solve this problem largely by the surplus created through production and commerce during World War II.[7]

SOCIO-SPATIAL STRUCTURE OF THE SHRINKING CITY

World War I, followed by the transformation of the sociopolitical system, was detrimental for the Ottoman ruling elite, who lost their functions and their privileged status. They no longer had the means to support their large households. Their great *konaks*, or mansions, in the old city of Istanbul—scattered in neighborhoods such as Süleymaniye, Vefa, Fatih, Sultanselim, Beyazıt, and Divanyolu—lost their grandeur and became deserted. These homes were soon divided up to house people of modest means who migrated from various parts of the dissolved Ottoman Empire (Tekeli 1992, p. 26).

The concentration of small and medium-sized industry along the banks of the Golden Horn—one of the major land-use decisions of the Prost Plan—contributed to the transformation of the social makeup of the old city. As workers and rural migrants settled within the old city, where manufacturing activity began to concentrate, areas near the Golden Horn developed as low-income neighborhoods. As neighborhoods in the historic city slid down the social ladder, the exodus of the better-off from the old city to the more prestigious neighborhoods on the northern banks of the Golden Horn intensified.

Pera and its environs continued to develop as fashionable residential areas, the first sign of a new kind of differentiation in space not only by ethno-religious origin but by class as well. Traditionally, in the neighborhoods of Istanbul, rich and poor lived side by side, and the *konaks* of the upper echelons of society were located amid more modest houses. Although ethno-religious groups tended to concentrate in certain neighborhoods, there were never clear demarcations separating these groups from one another, and it was commonplace to find Muslims and non-Muslims, elite and non-elite, living in the same areas (Artan 1989, Enlil 1994a).[8]

Pera/Beyoğlu also pioneered the emergence of a new housing type in the city: apartment buildings. Living in an apartment building soon became a status symbol for the emergent bourgeoisie and the younger generations of Muslim elite. By the turn of the century, apartment buildings had spread to other neighborhoods, becoming a fashionable form of housing in Şişli, Nişantaşı, and Teşvikiye.

Apartment buildings in the interwar years continued to be part of the cultural capital of the upper and upper-middle classes. For one thing, they were relatively expansive constructions compared to a simple two-story house. The great majority of apartment buildings were built for use value rather than exchange value, and in many cases the units were occupied by members of a family, with perhaps one or two apartments rented out. It took the immense population growth beginning in the 1950s and an acute shortage of housing before the construction of apartment buildings was truly commercialized and spread over the city as the dominant housing form for the majority.[9]

Squatter settlements, or *gecekondus,* also began to appear during the mid-1940s, although they would also become widespread after the 1950s. They emerged in proximity to the larger industrial establishments on the fringes as well as within the city near medium- and small-scale enterprises. By the 1950s, there were already patches of squatter areas in the old city and just outside ancient walls in areas such as Taşlıtarla,

Zeytinburnu, Beyoğlu, and elsewhere within municipal boundaries. The scale and extent of these early *gecekondus,* however, in no way matched developments in the following decades.

EXPLODING CITY: THE MAKING OF AN INDUSTRIAL METROPOLIS (1950–1980)

The postwar years witnessed a period of important social change in Turkey, marked by rapid industrialization and urbanization, which had crucial repercussions for Istanbul. Democratization of the political structure and the transition to a multiparty system was followed by a change of government through the elections of 1950. The policies pursued by the new liberal government gave the private sector a much more prominent role in economic development. Greater resources were allocated for industrial development, which initiated a new phase of industrialization and urbanization.

The pursuit of greater efficiency and commercialization in agriculture led to a considerable increase in the use of machinery. A significant loss of employment opportunities in rural Anatolia initiated the exodus of rural population from the countryside to rapidly flourishing industry. An emphasis on the development of motorways rather than railways enhanced the accessibility of major parts of the country.

In the 1960s Turkey, after ten years of liberalism, entered another phase of planned development under a dominant central government. The State Planning Organization was established in 1960. With the task of preparing national, sectoral, and regional development plans, the SPO was to identify subregions for priority of investment to promote more even distribution of development and more equitable income distribution. Within the mixed economic system adopted thereafter, the state and the private sector were expected to coordinate their activities with the national development plans and investment programs, which placed an emphasis on import-substitution-oriented rapid industrialization policy. This policy soon led to a growth rate of about 7 percent and the development of larger industrial complexes. Industrial growth, however, took place at the expense of the agricultural sector, exacerbating the massive migratory flows from rural areas.

Istanbul stood at the center of these changes; 65 percent of newly established enterprises were located there. Established infrastructure, a relatively large commodity market, and advantageous transportation facilities were influential factors. The momentum industrial development gained since the 1950s was intensified from the 1960s onward, and Istanbul became the country's engine. The majority of foreign capital chose Istanbul as the main site of investment.[10] Within the framework of the First and Second Five-Year National Development Plans, Istanbul, for the first time since the etatist era, received a large public investment in infrastructure. Istanbul also benefited the most from incentives to industrial development in the form of credits and aids. As a result, the number of both small- and large-scale industrial enterprises in Istanbul doubled between 1950 and 1964,[11] and increased by 82 percent from 1964 to 1972, with an increase in value added of 305 percent. In sum, only 20 percent of small- and large-scale industry was located in Istanbul in 1950; but by 1980 Istanbul was the center for 46 percent of industrial establishments in the country, employed 31 percent of industrial labor, and produced 33 percent of the value added.[12] By 1980, Istanbul was an "oversized industrial city" (Güvenç 1993), with large- and small-scale, labor-intensive manufacturing establishments that employed low-wage informal labor and absorbed manpower displaced from agriculture.

TRANSFORMATION OF SPATIAL STRUCTURE IN THE "CITY OF HOPE"

Economic development policies adopted since the early 1950s caused a massive exodus from rural areas, which overwhelmed major Turkish cities. Until then, only Ankara was growing at an annual rate of 6–6.5 percent. Istanbul was one of the major poles of attraction for the uprooted masses looking for job opportunities and better living conditions, and became a "city of hope" for millions. The population of the city, about 1 million in 1950, reached 2.2 million by 1970 and 2.9 million by 1980. The population of the metropolitan area, which was 1.1 million in 1950, became 3 million by 1970 and 4.7 million in 1980. These figures reflect the expansion of Istanbul beyond the city proper to lands at the periphery.

Until the 1970s, the urban form of Istanbul was determined by microclimatic conditions such as orientation toward the sun and prevailing winds, and its development was limited by natural boundaries such as forests and water bodies. Policies that gave priority to the construction of highways over railways, however, were soon to have an impact. The construction of the E-5 international motorway and the first bridge over the Bosphorus challenged the principles that had guided urban development for centuries and limited the expansion of the city.

Sprawl of industrial and residential areas in Istanbul during 1950-1980.
Source: Hüseyin Kaptan (1991a).

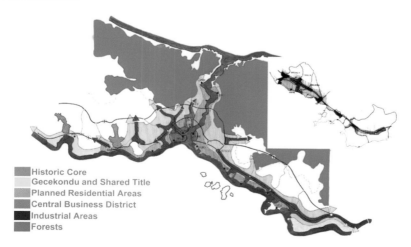

- Historic Core
- Gecekondu and Shared Title
- Planned Residential Areas
- Central Business District
- Industrial Areas
- Forests

Unplanned industrial development began to appear along the E-5 corridor, which extended parallel to the coasts of the Marmara Sea and 2–3 kilometers inland from the coastline on both the European and Asian sides of the city. These industrial areas were soon followed by housing for the working classes and urban poor, which were illegal and outside any planning regulations, as were the industrial developments themselves (Kaptan 1988). The first bridge over the Bosphorus and its freeway system was put into service in 1973 without any cost-benefit analysis. Furthermore, insufficient regulation controlled land uses surrounding the bridge and its access network. The bridge triggered the sprawl of the city not only in an east-west direction but also toward the north. Hence the urban form of Istanbul was altered and the city began to grow in spite of all the natural boundaries, threatening natural resources that needed protection (Yenen et al. 1993).

Agricultural lands surrounding the city were opened for urban development, and the ratio of population living within the 10-kilometer ring dropped by 20 percent between 1960 and 1980. In 1960, the urbanized areas on both the European and Asian sides of the city extended 30 kilometers from the center. This distance grew to 40 kilometers in 1970 and 50 kilometers in 1980 (Sengezer and Enlil 1999). Today it stretches about 80 kilometers to the west and 40 kilometers to the east.[13]

The Anatolian side of the city received a large share of this urban sprawl and developed very rapidly. Within ten years, the summer resorts composed of magnificent mansions were transformed into year-round residences surrounded by high-density apartment buildings. Yet the central business district and main working areas were still concentrated on the European side, causing increasing commuter traffic. The people of Istanbul have always created their suburbs away from the city center, using ferries and suburban trains in their daily commute to work. This pattern was changed, however, after the bridge was constructed. Today, hours spent commuting via the two bridges has become a part of daily life. Incentives given to the automotive industry and to private car ownership have contributed to this relationship between the European and Anatolian sides of Istanbul.[14]

NEW ALLIANCES AND EMERGENT SOCIO-SPATIAL FORMS

The massive migratory flows, which put urgent demands on housing, were not, however, coupled with public policy to meet the needs of the masses. In the absence of sound housing policies, the migrants who poured into the cities improvised their own shelter. On publicly owned lands, they built *gecekondus*. These informal settlements, which increasingly took hold on the fringe of cities, were seen as part of the housing problem that afflicted the country since World War II. Policies to overcome housing shortages were mainly targeted to middle- and upper-middle-income groups. Efforts to provide low-income housing were limited and ineffective.

Although demolitions were undertaken from time to time, the *gecekondu* population was generally seen as a great source of votes, especially given the clientelistic nature of urban politics from the 1950s onward. Thus amnesties were granted from

Gecekondu belts surrounding the city. Photo: Hüseyin Kaptan.

time to time, before or after elections, legalizing the illegally built settlements.[15]
Policies veered between prohibition, demolition, and legalization, creating an atmosphere of uncertainty that encouraged migrants to continue building *gecekondus*
because there was always the hope of land ownership. Once a title to land was
obtained through acts of amnesty, it did not take long for poor migrants to convert
small houses into apartment buildings. Thus they were provided not only with secured

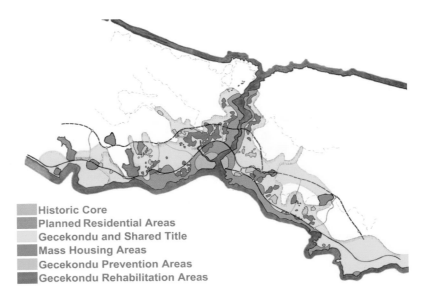

Historic Core
Planned Residential Areas
Gecekondu and Shared Title
Mass Housing Areas
Gecekondu Prevention Areas
Gecekondu Rehabilitation Areas

Legal status of residential areas in Istanbul. Source: Hüseyin Kaptan (1991a).

rights to ownership but also with new sources of income through apartments for sale or rent within an inflationary economy (Enlil et al. 1998), which became a significant means of economic mobility (Öncü 1988).

Initially the *gecekondu* was a form of housing that met the urgent shelter needs of low-income rural migrants. It became commercialized over time, and a market dominated by "squatter lords" was formed when the owners of capital, whether land or cash, realized the lucrative market the provision of relatively cheap land for housing could offer. A way was invented to produce land for residential development: in "split-deed ownership," or *hisseli ifraz,* large tracts of agricultural land on the periphery was split into very small deeds and sold to newcomers.[16] Squatter housing thus obtained a partially secure status whereby the ownership of land was legal but construction upon it was not, because building on the cheap lands outside of planning boundaries was not allowed. From the mid-1970s onward, the possibilities of seizing publicly owned vacant land at the periphery were almost exhausted, and the newcomers had no choice but to pay large sums to buy split-deed plots lying on the outskirts of the city. Today more than half of Istanbul's population lives in illegally formed housing, whether *gecekondus* occupying publicly owned lands or split-deed settlements (Öncü 1988, Enlil and Dinçer 1999).

Given limited opportunities for upward mobility for the migrants, either through marginal-sector jobs or as low-paid public-sector employees and industrial workers, exploiting opportunities provided by the informal land market was the only way out of poverty. For the governments, sustaining this status of uncertainty assured the loyalty of the masses in a context of urban politics largely dominated by clientelistic relations and patronage. In the absence of policies for the provision of low-income housing, the process involved a tacit alliance between the actors who had a formal say in building the urban environment and those who actually built it.

Scarcity of urban land in the planned sections of the city, mounting need for housing in the face of increasing population, and skyrocketing land values led to another form of improvised housing production frequently referred to as "build and sell" *(yap-sat)*. This involved collaboration between urban landowners and small capital owners or even contractors with no capital other than their organizing capacity, who acted as middlemen between landowners and potential buyers. The system rested on the scarcity of resources of all parties involved: landowner, entrepreneur, and potential buyer. The landowner did not have the means to undertake the costly production of a larger building; the entrepreneur did not have enough capital (if any) to buy urban land and construct a building on it. Therefore an agreement was reached between the landowner and the entrepreneur, in which they pooled their limited resources to capitalize on rising urban land values and transform the city: the landowner provided the land; whatever existed on it was demolished and an apartment building was constructed. Depending on the deal, the landowner got a certain share of the apartments and the entrepreneur got the rest. Usually the units were sold during the process and helped finance construction. This mode of building involved the relatively smaller parcels in the city where there were modest single-family houses, as well as those on which stood mansions of the Ottoman era, whether in the city *(konak)* or in the summer resorts *(köşk)* located especially on the Anatolian side of the city.

Apartment buildings provided a form of housing that responded to worsening shortages. Soon a legal framework for the ownership of apartments was needed. The Condominium Law, enacted in 1958 and amended in 1965, gave momentum to the construction of apartment buildings. The face of the city was significantly changed within not more than two decades. Through this ruthless process of renewal, the traditional urban fabric of wooden houses and mansions was largely torn down to make way for much denser neighborhoods of apartment buildings, deemed modern and more convenient.

Thus between 1950 and 1980, all sectors of society rushed to build and strove to gain something from the highly speculative land market. Long-term societal benefits were sacrificed to short-term economic gains, and Istanbul exploded beyond the previous limits that defined its urban form both horizontally and vertically. While the inner-city neighborhoods were renewed largely at the expense of the historic urban fabric and became much denser, the city overall sprawled at the expense of natural resources such as forests, water basins, and agricultural lands.

FRAGMENTED CITY: DILEMMAS OF GLOBAL ASPIRATIONS (1980–2005)

In the 1980s, Turkey was pulled into the currents of globalization. This period was marked by neoliberal economic policies geared to open the national economy to world markets. The policies, which commenced with the austerity measures of 24 January

1981, were aimed at replacing the import-substituting economy of the previous decades with one geared to exports. These policies brought structural changes: to banking and the stock exchange, in taxation and the introduction of trade zones, in a push toward the convertibility of the Turkish lira, in the privatization of public-sector enterprises, and in new regulations concerning local administrations (Kaptan 1991, p. 9). After direct military rule between 1980 and 1983, the ANAP government that came to power under the leadership of Turgut Özal in 1983 took measures toward deregulation and the diminution of the role of the state, to encourage a free-market economy.

In its political strategy, ANAP reconciled an uncompromising market ideology with the populism that prevailed in Turkish politics, successfully replacing the rural populism of the previous era with urban populism (Keyder and Öncü 1994, p. 398). In this way, ANAP departed from the dominant political discourse of right-wing parties since the 1950s, which gained political power by appealing to the rural electorate. In big cities such as Istanbul, ANAP aimed to appeal to all major groups within society (Enlil et al. 1998). The government adapted three major policies regarding metropolitan areas. First, new legal provisions allowed metropolitan administrations to increase revenues by levying new taxes and increasing existing ones. New financial opportunities were thus created for cities to invest in large-scale infrastructure projects. Second, state funding for mass housing projects was provided through the creation of the Mass Housing Fund (MHF) and the Mass Housing Administration (MHA), and Istanbul was the major recipient of these funds. Third, new legislation prompted the creation of a two-tiered metropolitan government model for the three cities of the Turkish Triangle: Ankara, Istanbul, and Izmir. The new model transferred authority for coordination and administrative action from the bureaucracies of the central government to the three metropolitan municipalities. The model also introduced a second tier of district municipalities, each with its own elected mayor and municipal council. All planning powers were also decentralized and vested with the district municipalities, which had a great impact on shaping the built environment.[17]

TRANSFORMATION OF THE URBAN STRUCTURE IN THE NEW ERA OF INTERNATIONALISM

The legal, financial, and institutional restructuring of the early 1980s created a climate favorable for making Istanbul an international service city (Kaptan 1991, p. 9). Istanbul emerged as the focal point of the neoliberal policies and the new strategy of integrating the national economy with global markets. Slowly, the economic base began to change. Although about one-third of Turkish industry was still located in the Istanbul metropolitan area, from 1980 to 1990 there was a notable shift from manufacturing to finance and services (Aksoy 1996, p. 11). With an employment growth rate of 117 percent, producer services were the fastest-growing sectors in Istanbul; employment in finance increased by 37 percent, insurance by 36 percent, and real estate and business services by 220 percent.[18] During the same period, consumer services and retailing activities rose by 65.5 percent and 77.5 percent respectively (Aksoy 1996, p. 21).

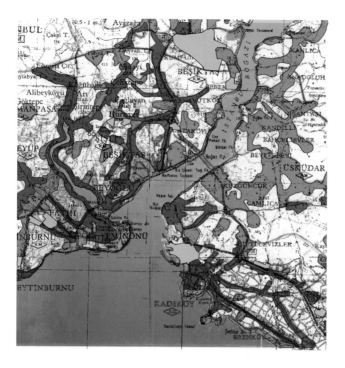

Residential
Commerce & Business
Industry
Public Services
Military Academy
Green Areas
Culture & Tourism

Land-use pattern in the central areas of Istanbul, before (above) and after (below) 1980. Note the expansion after 1980 toward the north on the European side and toward the east on the Anatolian side, replacing the former industrial areas.
Source: Hüseyin Kaptan (1991a).

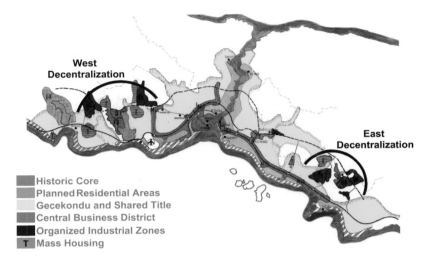

West
Decentralization

East
Decentralization

Historic Core
Planned Residential Areas
Gecekondu and Shared Title
Central Business District
Organized Industrial Zones
T Mass Housing

Decentralization of industry to "Organized Industrial Areas" on the outskirts.
Source: Hüseyin Kaptan (1991a).

Beginning in 1983, structural changes to attract international capital resulted in a significant increase in foreign direct investment. Between 1980 and 1998, FDI in Turkey increased 320 times, with a sharp increase especially after 1990. The share of manufacturing in FDIs decreased from 91.5 percent to 62.0 percent, while that of the service sector rose from 8.4 percent to 36.7 percent (Özdemir 2002, p. 252). About 60 percent of total FDI and 95 percent of banking and finance was located in Istanbul (Özdemir 2000, p. 98).[19] Thus Istanbul absorbed much of this flow and emerged as the prime target of foreign capital.

Economic transformations were reflected in urban space; Istanbul was the showcase of the country's new era of internationalism. Part of this agenda was to enhance the image of the city and brand it in the international arena. Istanbul aspired to host global functions and welcome conventions, businesspeople, and wealthy tourists. This was to be done by improving urban spaces, facilities, and infrastructure and by providing quality office spaces and luxurious hotels to meet the expectations of transnational capital.

Numerous modern office towers, convention centers, exhibition and fair grounds, and deluxe hotels were built. The Act on the Promotion of Tourism, enacted in 1982, allowed the central government to declare certain strategic sites "tourism centers," with incentives such as credits, tax deductions, and exemptions from customs duties granted to investors. The Act vested all planning powers for these areas with the central government, which could bypass local planning regulations and grant increased building rights. It did not take long to use the provisions of this law to grant special building rights to uses other than tourism, especially in the expanded central business district, where there was strong demand by international finance organizations and

New skyline of Istanbul with new office buildings at the background and Swiss Hotel in the foreground.
Source: galeri.istanbul.gov.tr; Photo: Faruk Kocak.

other business headquarters. Between 1984 and 1993, forty areas were declared tourism or "tourism and business" centers, which promoted the building of high-rise office towers and deluxe hotels (Ekinci 1993, p. 21). The central business district extended toward the north along the Büyükdere-Maslak axis, as new high-rise office towers were built. It was mainly here that banking and other financial services, trading companies, and headquarters of national and multinational firms began to locate in the mid-1980s, a process that gained momentum during the 1990s. While the Büyükdere-Maslak axis became the prominent business district of the city in the new era of internationalism, the Eminönü and Beyoğlu districts in the historical core lost their dominance as centers of finance, banking, insurance, real estate, and company headquarters (Özdemir 2002). This process had begun in the late 1960s, when congestion in these areas and the increasing demand for space by the service sector became a problem. An exodus ensued toward new areas along Taksim-Şişli-Zincirlikuyu-Mecidiyeköy and the Beşiktaş-Barbaros Boulevard axis.[20] The expansion of the CBD toward the north was facilitated by the significant transformations since the 1980s. The installment of two bridges over the Bosphorus (one in the early 1970s and the other in the early 1980s), with their corresponding access roads, played a major role in this expansion. These bridges increased the accessibility of the areas along the Büyükdere-Maslak axis from either side of the Bosphorus and from the international airport. In addition, the construction of a metro system between Taksim and Levent, however short by international standards, increased the accessibility of the area to the cultural core in and around Taksim and in the district of Beyoğlu, which is still part of the CBD. The policy of clearing industry from the city to make way for the service sector contributed to the development of the Büyükdere-Maslak axis, along which there were many former industrial sites.[21] Within

New business district along the Büyükdere-Maslak axis. Photo: Talat Enlil.

two decades, the skyline of Istanbul was crowded with office towers rivaling (and jeopardizing, many believed) the renowned traditional skyline of the city.

Numerous luxury hotels constructed during this period feature magnificent views of the Bosphorus. Swissôtel the Bosphorus, built upon the grounds of the Dolmabahçe Palace, Çırağan Palace Kempinski, sited on the grounds of the Çırağan Palace, and other international chains such as Ritz-Carlton, Conrad Istanbul, Mövenpick, and Hyatt Regency were part of the agenda to promote tourism and increase the five-star hotel capacity of Istanbul. These hotels were either high-rises or simply massive buildings, creating large patches in the fine-grain urban fabric of the city. Until the 1980s, there were only four structures exceeding twenty stories in Istanbul. Within a decade, more than twenty new tall structures—all hotels and office buildings—were built. By the 2000s, their numbers had already more than doubled, epitomizing the rapidly flourishing sectors of the economy (Keyder and Öncü 1994).

High-rise development was only one of the components attesting to Istanbul's aspirations for global status. Deliberate building programs were undertaken to enhance the connectivity of the city and increase its competitiveness in the international arena. Istanbul received a major influx of state funding in spite of austerity measures and a general decline in state subsidies. Numerous megaprojects were undertaken, including the installation of the second bridge over the Bosphorus with the accompanying Trans-European Motorway, enlargement and improvement of the Atatürk International Airport, and the building of a new international airport on the Anatolian side.

Supporting this agenda were extensive urban renewal projects carried out under the entrepreneurial leadership of Mayor Bedrettin Dalan. Dalan embodied the figure of a mayor quite unknown until then. Aided by the new financial possibilities granted to metropolitan governments, he deployed executive power to the greatest possible extent, often "with rapid action preceding bureaucratic paperwork, and little patience for legal procedure or for canons of historical preservation" (Keyder and Öncü 1994, p. 408). Among the ambitious projects he undertook during the five years he was in office

(1984–89) were: opening major thoroughfares within the city, such as the Tarlabaşı Boulevard, by an intensive clearing of the city's nineteenth-century inner-city neighborhoods; building up wide avenues along the shores of the Marmara, and the controversial coastal road on the European side of the Bosphorus; and numerous other interventions made to the urban fabric to enhance the inner-city transportation network. One of the most controversial projects undertaken by Dalan was the clearing of industry from the shores of the Golden Horn. This operation was in line with the general policy of removing unsightly industry from the city. It also coincided with the project sponsored by the World Bank for cleaning the waters of the Golden Horn and restoring its legendary past with fresh, blue waters and green shores. This was a radical operation through which thousands of buildings were bulldozed and many small manufacturing firms evicted. The waters of the Golden Horn were cleaned to some extent and unsightly buildings replaced by lawns and parks; but the feverish demolitions done in haste, without an inventory, also resulted in the loss of a considerable number of historic buildings that were part of the city's industrial heritage.

Istanbul's linkages with the global economy were also manifest in the emergence of new commercial activity. Until the 1980s, retail activities were dominated by traditional small-scale traders; multinational retail firms were almost nonexistent.[22] The shift toward large-scale companies involved foreign as well as domestic corporations (Tokatlı and Boyacı 1999). Benefiting from the new economic and legal arrangements of the early 1980s, foreign retailers began to enter the Turkish market in the early 1990s. The rising population of Istanbul, already exceeding 7 million in 1990, provided a sizeable and steady consumer market; 60 percent of the foreign firms that invested in Istanbul were retailers. While there were 1,158 foreign retail firms in 1998, powerful capital holders in industry and finance invested in the lucrative real-estate market, mainly in office buildings and shopping centers with significant spatial imprints on the city (Özdemir 2002).

As domestic and foreign corporations, with or without joint ventures, entered the retail market in Istanbul, shopping centers and hypermarkets began to appear. German Metro AG, Real Adler, Praktiker, Götzen, Bauhaus, Mr. Bricolage, Carrefoure, and Ikea are some examples. The Galleria shopping center was opened in 1998 in Bakırköy district, the first of its kind, and drew shoppers from the whole city (Özdemir 2002). It was not long, however, before its privileged status was shaken by rival shopping centers. Atrium, Akmerkez, Capitol, and Carousel all opened in the early 1990s, Metrocity, Nautilus, and Kanyon in the 2000s.

Starting with the ubiquitous McDonald's and Benetton, international chains also became widespread. Fast-food chains such as Burger King, Kentucky Fried Chicken, Pizza Hut, Domino's Pizza, Schlotsky's, and Dunkin' Donuts soon became commonplace, followed by various domestic chains. A similar trend could be observed in the spread of retail chains such as Toys "R" Us, Marks & Spencer, Zara, Mango, Stefanel, Lacoste, and Tommy Hilfiger, to cite only a few. Upscale retailers such as Armani, Burberry's, Gucci, Max Mara, DNKY, and Hugo Boss arrived in the city in the late 1990s and clustered in the fashionable neighborhood of Nişantaşı.

Another trend has been the development of a café culture, through both local initiatives that flourished since the mid-1980s and the entry of international chains such as Gloria Jean's and Starbucks into the market in the 2000s, along with the emergence of domestic chains such as Kahve Dünyası.

These transformations were signs of the emergence of a new consumer culture and that "Istanbul's economy was now firmly linked to the developed economies of Europe and the rest of the world" (Tokatlı and Boyacı 1999, p. 188).

EMERGENT SOCIO-SPATIAL FORMS IN THE FRAGMENTED CITY

Until the 1980s, Istanbul had a rather clear socio-spatial geography, a general pattern of settlement where a belt of upper- and upper-middle-class residential areas followed the shorelines of the Marmara Sea and the Bosphorus, and a second belt of middle-income housing developed between this first belt and the E-5 highway.[23] There were no sharp differences between the residential patterns of the upper- and middle-income groups: although certain residential addresses signaled prestige, both groups lived in apartment houses in the planned sections of the city mostly built through the "build and sell" process in reasonably heterogeneous residential neighborhoods. A third belt beyond the E-5 was almost solely composed of *gecekondus* and split-deed housing of lower-income rural migrants. This pattern, however, began to change significantly since the 1980s, and Istanbul witnessed the emergence of new socio-spatial formations partitioning the city into compartments, a process that continues today (Enlil 2005).

A number of factors contributed to this dynamic and the resultant socio-spatial forms. First, the population of Istanbul continued to increase. The population of the city was 4.7 million in 1980; it reached 7.3 million in 1990 and 10 million in 2000. The steady increase in population put pressures on the housing market. As urban land within the planned sections of the city became scarce, the production costs of *yap-sat* increased, putting strains on this model of production, a major means of housing supply for the middle-income groups. Indeed, the production of housing decreased by half in the first half of the 1980s.[24] Meanwhile, public lands on which *gecekondus* were built were almost exhausted. Second, neoliberal policies pursued since the 1980s led to the emergence of new societal groups with high incomes and firm ties to international business who acted as agents of both global taste and polarization of income, which sharpened inequalities.

MASS HOUSING SCHEMES: HOMOGENEOUS PATCHES ON THE PERIPHERY

In the context of decreased housing production despite population growth, the ANAP government intervened in the housing market despite its free-market ideology.[25] In 1984, the government amended the Mass Housing Act of 1981, founded the MHA, and launched the MHF. Through these funds, the government aimed to provide housing for middle- and lower-middle-income groups. In the following years, there was a significant increase in housing production and, between 1984 and 1991, more than 100,000 units were constructed in Istanbul through MHF in areas designated for mass housing (Keyder and Öncü 1993, p. 33). Large tracts of land, especially along the main highways, were developed as mass housing settlements built almost exclusively as identical high-rise apartment blocks. The city began to grow by the addition of these large fragments on the periphery, in contrast to the patterns of *yap-sat* production, which was piece-meal city building on a lot-by-lot basis by small capital holders. This production was organized as housing cooperatives, formed either by the developers themselves or by associations of employees, retirees, etc.[26] By the early 1990s, through the new mecha-nisms, the housing sector became a profitable area of investment for large capital hold-ers. For these powerful actors, investment in the lucrative urban land and real estate markets was increasingly attractive, and they began to invest in the construction of hotels and office towers as well as housing.

Mass housing projects forming ribbons of high-rise, high-density suburbs on the periphery created socially more homogeneous residential environments as middle-income groups and upwardly mobile *gecekondu* residents moved from their older neigh-borhoods. These new socio-spatial developments were a harbinger of a more polarized and fragmented social landscape that would emerge within the next few years.[27]

EXPANSION OF THE "ILLEGAL CITY"

Alongside an effort to build housing through public funds was an equally significant rush to build in the newly established district municipalities. The great majority of this development was illegal and took place by the opening of large tracts of agricultural land to split-deed or shared-title developments. Influential in the spread of this new wave of illegal, unhealthy development were clientelistic relations and alliances among the newly elected councilmen and their largely immigrant constituencies. These rela-tions resulted in the formation of an "illegal city" in the newly annexed lands on the periphery through networks of councilmen, contractors, and settlers.[28] Place of origin was at the center of these networks, creating neighborhoods characterized by ethno-cultural cleavages (Keyder and Öncü 1994, pp. 410–411).

The building boom and the rapid spread of illegal developments brought in their wake a new series of amnesties.[29] What differentiated these new acts from those enact-ed before the 1980s was not only their scope but also their content. The pre-1980s amnesties were granted only to *gecekondus* built on public land; offering ownership rights and increased building rights was not included. The new laws extended the scope of amnesties to include split-deed or shared-title developments, legalizing construction. The Act of 1984 introduced the concept of "rehabilitation plan" through which environ-mental quality was to be improved in the vast spread of the "illegal city" where there was not enough infrastructure and public facilities. The Act granted the right to build up to four stories, initiating a rapid process of rebuilding. The resultant transformation was, however, far from the aims of improved environmental quality. A provision stated that existing conditions should be taken into account, and that standards as set in the

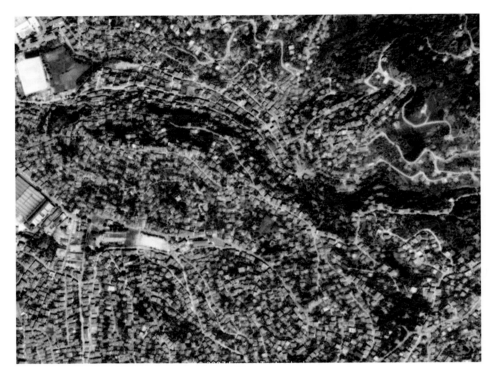

Spread of illegal *gecekondu* settlements. Source: Google Earth.

The amnesties resulted in the densification of illegal settlements.
Source: Baraka Art, Wikipedia.

Building Law for facilities such as parks, schools, and other public areas were not applicable everywhere. In an economy of rampant inflation and rising land values, this provision undermined efforts to enhance urban quality (Enlil et al. 1998). Instead it was instrumental in legalizing the mechanisms of urban rent and opening new channels of accumulation for those involved in the reproduction of the urban environment, including the migrants who instantly converted their houses to multistory apartment buildings.[30]

Yet for new generations of migrants, the chance of seizing similar opportunities on the periphery has diminished. Land has become a scarce commodity, as powerful sectors of society are vying for land on the periphery. Moreover, local politicians are no longer as committed to populism and instead seek opportunities to transform their districts to play a more significant role in the globalizing city.

"GATED CITIES" OF THE NEW ELITE

The appearance of gated communities in the city paralleled the emergence of a new upper strata of corporate executives and professionals. This new elite, whose aspirations as well as income have risen significantly since the 1980s, had particular demands for housing. They wanted homes away from the chaos and crowds of the city, apart from with others with whom they did not want to mix, and a certain lifestyle. Thus cracks began to appear in the socio-spatial formation of the city as the upper strata began to move to gated communities (Enlil 2005).[31]

These residential developments were initially groups of villas on the hills overlooking the Bosphorus or luxurious apartment buildings in the suburbs with easy access to the newly flourishing CBD.[32] Protected by high walls and gate security, they isolated themselves from the surrounding middle-class apartment buildings and *gecekondus*.

Spread of gated communities in the Istanbul Metropolitan Area. Source: Adapted from IMP Housing and Quality of Life Group, 2006.

Later examples of central-city gated communities or "citadels," in Marcuse's terms (1999), include luxurious apartments in towers built as part of a shopping center and office complex such as Akmerkez and Metro City. Other "tower residences" are built solely as residential developments, yet designed to provide the comforts of a deluxe hotel.

As the ranks of Istanbul's new elites swelled, the number of gated communities also increased. They rapidly spread along the outskirts of the city, previously the domain of the *gecekondus*. The two classes had never been spatially so close yet socially so far apart. Before, all had used the same streets, shopped at the same corner grocery store, took their children to the same parks, and used the same public facilities. In the new gated city, there were walls, guards, and high-tech surveillance systems. As Keyder and Öncü state, in the Istanbul of the post-1980s, "a villa became the prime indicator of bourgeois status" (1994, p. 410). These "dream houses" came with ameneties such as fitness centers, social clubs, sports grounds and swimming pools, and day-care centers. Some included artificial ponds set amid green parks, golf courses, and horse-riding facilities (Kemer Country); others had cinemas on their grounds (Acar Kent). Thus residents had no reason to go out unless they really wanted to; everything was provided, and life inside these gated communities was "totalized" (Enlil 2003b and 2005). A green and "clean" environment—both physically and socially—made the gated cities attractive to people who wished to distance themselves from the rest of society (Öncü 1997, Enlil 2003b and 2005).[33]

Citadels of the new elite. In the foreground is the recently completed Kanyon project, which includes a shopping mall, entertainment court, office building, and luxurious apartments. In the background is the Metrocity Millennium Project, which includes a shopping mall, twin towers of luxurious residences, and an office tower. Photo: Nazlı Han.

The middle classes followed the new elite and created their own gated communities on the periphery amid the illegal settlements. Source: www.dumankaya.com.

"Mashattan" Project in Maslak. Note the industrial park in the background to the left and informal *gecekondu* settlements beyond extending toward the Bosphorus. Source: www.tasyapi.com/projeler.

In an effort to imitate the lifestyles and housing patterns of the elite and to increase their status,[34] the middle classes of Istanbul began to move to gated settlements on the periphery.[35] Their gated residences, however, were more modest and composed of high-rise apartment blocks instead of fancy villas. This exodus from the city's older neighborhoods and suburbs reached its apex after the earthquake in 1999, as many upper- and middle-class families began to flee their homes, which were perceived as disaster prone. This flight was toward the north, to the attractive forest areas and water basins, jeopardizing the natural resources of the city. Luxury housing complexes such as "Almond Hill," "Novus Residences," "Incity," and the most pretentious, "Mashattan," are being built in the older suburbs of the city, changing the social topography and physical layout.

"ABANDONED CITY" OF THE POOR AND EXCLUDED

These new settlements amid forests and greenery or with magnificent views of the Bosphorus represented in some ways the bright side of globalization since the 1980s. Yet they also hightlight the increasing gap between rich and poor, which is most evident in the run-down, poverty-stricken historic quarters (Enlil 2003b).

Since the turn of the twentieth century, the prestigious neighborhoods in the historic core—the Istanbul peninsula on the southern banks of the Golden Horn and Galata and Beyoğlu on its northern banks—have steadily been abandoned by their

Use of public space in Tarlabaşı—streets as a playground for kids. Photo: Zeynep Enlil.

original inhabitants, who moved to more fashionable new neighborhoods such as Şişli and Nişantaşı. But the real change occurred after the mid-1950s and 1960s as the majority of residents moved either to newly developing prestigious neighborhoods further to the north or to the suburbs on the Asian side; others left the country.[36] The deserted historic quarters were taken up by successive waves of migrants from rural Anatolia, who either bought or rented property or simply took refuge in the derelict buildings.[37]

Until very recently, poverty in Turkish cities has largely been associated with the population that migrated from rural areas to cities and settled in the periphery, forming a belt of squatter areas. Yet the history of urbanization in Istanbul over the last half-century provides us with examples of migrants who succeeded in overcoming poverty.[38] These success stories were largely a result of informal networks established in labor as well as housing markets, which compensated for the lack of sufficient welfare-state mechanisms. The residents of the run-down historic districts of the city were mostly rural migrants who could not afford the informal housing market on the periphery.[39] They were excluded from the formal and informal networks that provided opportunities for social mobility (Dinçer and Enlil 2003).

Structural changes since the 1980s, together with deindustrialization of the city, meant that the new generations of migrants, especially those in historic neighborhoods at the center, had much less opportunity to get manufacturing jobs.[40] If they were able to get a job, they were employed in low-paid, temporary jobs in the service sector, mostly in personal services, or they swelled the ranks of the marginal sector as peddlers and street vendors. Besides the migrants, the residents of the historic core included those born in Istanbul. According to a study done in Tarlabaşı, one of the most dilapidated neighborhoods in Beyoğlu, the unemployment rate was the highest among them; and other indicators such as homeownership and income level were the lowest.[41] All residents of this neighborhood lived below the poverty line. In this sense, they form a social group of "new urban poor" in Turkish cities, akin to the "underclass" in cities of the West.[42] Yet in the "abandoned city" occupied by the poor, the unemployed, and others excluded from society, there is a vivid social life. In these forsaken quarters, neighborly relations help residents cope with poverty (Enlil 2003b).

THE GENTRIFIED CITY

Another city is emerging at the core next to the abandoned city, most significantly in the Beyoğlu district, where gentrification is already under way. Gentrification is a latecomer to Istanbul compared to western counterparts, starting in the 1980s as a sporadic phenomenon in neighborhoods such as Kuzguncuk on the Anatolian banks of the Bosphorus and in Cihangir, on the southern slopes of Beyoğlu. A handful of artists and intellectuals were the pioneers of this process.[43]

In Beyoğlu, gentrification began in and around Istiklal Boulevard, which was turned into a grand pedestrian way with an old-fashioned tramcar running in the middle, reminiscent of the nineteenth century. Known as the Grand Rue de Pera in the nineteenth century, this axis has been the cultural and commercial hub of the city since then, despite a period of decline starting in the 1950s.[44] A historic district such as Beyoğlu could not go unnoticed given the aspiration of raising Istanbul's status in the global arena. Pedestrianization of the boulevard was a first step in reviving the glory of the district. Nostalgia for this storied period was evidenced in literary works, films, television programs, and exhibitions, as well as in editorials and features in newspapers and magazines. The interest in the city's pre-Republican history was also clearly manifest in academic research.

Beyoğlu's cinemas and theaters were revived; fancy cafés, restaurants and wine bars, bookstores, art galleries, and antique stores were opened. Instrumental in this process of revival were the internationally accredited music, film, jazz, and theater festivals, and the Istanbul Biennale. The number of art galleries and cultural centers also

A controversial renovation project in Cezayir Street, which involved the displacement of residents and the creation of a "themed" environment. The street was renamed as the "French Street"; all cafés and restaurants were to serve French cuisine. However, it proved to be commercially infeasible; now the restaurants serve a variety of cuisines and the name of the street was changed back to its original due to heated criticism. Photo: Senem Kozaman.

Renovated buildings in Beyoğlu. Photo: Zeynep Enlil.

Art Gallery on Istiklal. Within the context of the 9th Istanbul Biennale, this exhibition featured replicas of the four horses that once stood in the Hippodrome of Constantinople and were taken to St. Mark's Basilica in Venice in 1204 during the fourth crusades which sacked the city. Photo: Senem Kozaman.

increased significantly. Finance-sector players, such as Akbank, Yapı Kredi Bank, and Garanti Bank, as well as large holding companies such as Borusan, were the leaders of this process (Enlil 2000b). As a result, many nineteenth-century buildings were renovated and put to a variety of uses. The "new cultural classes"[45] began to occupy quarters such as Asmalımescit, Çukurcuma, and Galata[46] as their places of residence, work, and play (Enlil 2000b).

Real estate agents and investors were quick to realize the lucrative potential of the historic building stock. To take advantage of the rent gap,[47] they began to buy up property to renovate and sell for a significant profit. Two recent developments compound these trends and contribute to the escalation of property values in Beyoğlu. First, new legal arrangements allow property ownership by foreigners. Second, a new act on the renewal historic building stock endows local authorities with the power to revive historic areas, mainly to promote tourism. Istanbul has become a rising star in international real estate markets.[48] These trends add to the displacement of current residents by pricing them out of the market (Islam and Enlil 2006).

EPILOGUE: LOOKING TOWARD THE FUTURE

From even this brief account of Istanbul's history of urban development, it is apparent that a unique city such as Istanbul, with its historical, cultural, and natural assets, and its aspirations for global status, is bound to face a number of dilemmas. Global positioning strategies could contribute to reprofiling the city and increasing its competitive edge, yet can these strategies be reconciled with healthy, sustainable urban development that respects the urban rights of all citizens? Who pays the costs of integration with global markets? Planning is a redistributive act; who wins and who loses? And how should the city address the increasing income polarization prompted by globalization? How can further social polarization and exclusion that leads to the formation of a highly fragmented city be prevented? How can the already fragmented parts of the city be integrated? Other major challenges include reconciling conflicts between the economy and ecology, and protecting the historic heritage of the city to prevent further damage to its historic fabric and renowned skyline.

These are not easy problems that can be solved by spatial planning alone. Yet some fundamental principles could be delineated if Istanbul desires a sustainable future and a socially just society. First, Istanbul can no longer afford mindless exploitation of its natural resources. This is as true for poor migrants as it is for the new rich of the city who seek a protected life behind gates amid forests or along protected water basins. The natural context for urban development—the forests, water resources, and natural drainage systems—should be zealously protected. Istanbul can no longer sacrifice ecology to economy. The same holds true for the famous skyline of Istanbul. There should be an end to skyscrapers vying with this unique historic heritage, and the misuse of historic building stock.

There should be a limit to the growth of Istanbul. Inasmuch as this involves broader national and regional policies to prevent or slow migration to the city, regional cooperation should be sought to alleviate population pressures. Decentralization of industry to the outskirts of the city-region seems to be a key factor. Many examples from all over the world, however, have shown clearly that deindustrialization results in severe employment and that the replacement of industry with services does not necessarily create jobs for former industrial workers. Thus it is important that industrial decentralization be carefully planned and phased, with accompanying policies and programs to minimize unemployment. On the other hand, if Istanbul is going to have a competitive edge in the global economy that is increasingly becoming knowledge driven, it is inevitable that the industrial base of the city needs to be modernized and restructured toward more competitive and high-tech industries. This requires well-organized and comprehensive efforts to enhance human capital.

Given the monocentric structure of Istanbul, there is a need to identify subregions and clusters within the metropolitan area for the planning of a multicentered and balanced settlement system. A hierarchical ranking of centers within the metropolitan system is urgent given the highly imbalanced structure, which is at the root of the heavy commuter traffic, particularly acute between the two sides of the Bosphorus. A spatial and functional balance between the European and Anatolian sides in terms of the distribution of residential areas and workplaces seems essential. Such a spatial policy should be coupled with the provision of housing, urban services, and facilities in the newly industrialized areas or organized industrial zones.

Other equally important challenges include increasing the quality of residential areas through rehabilitation and providing quality housing for residents now living in earthquake-prone areas. Renewal of the building stock to make it earthquake resistant is not easy given dense development. Complicating the issue is the ownership structure, with thousands of individual titles. Nevertheless, the renewal of these areas is an urgent matter toward which a considerable amount of public resources should be allocated, and new instruments to facilitate renewal should be devised.

Another crucial issue concerns the "soft" spaces in the city such as former industrial sites, dockyards, warehouses, and waterfronts, all occupying valuable lands at the center. They constitute attractive locations for redevelopment for both national and international investors. As in many other cities, redevelopment schemes for such areas in Istanbul are usually envisaged as iconic projects such as office towers, deluxe hotels, and shopping centers. Flagship projects do have the potential to trigger the local economy and make the city attractive for capital, yet when realized as piecemeal projects, without an eye to the urban context as a whole, such megaprojects can do more harm than good. Numerous examples in Istanbul over the past two decades burdened existing infrastructure and competed with the skyline. These glittering megaprojects also tend to provoke tension between actors in society, especially when they are brought onto the public agenda top-down, without regard for local plans and metropolitan planning studies already under way, or for public sensitivities. Controversies arise when the content or location of projects conflicts with expectations of benefit for the public at large. For Istanbul to claim global standing, having a sustainable and livable city for all citizens should be the major public policy priority.

A great challenge lies ahead for decision makers who seek to balance these two opposing forces.

References

Aksoy, A. (1996). *Küreselleşme ve İstanbul'da İstihdam.* İstanbul: Fes.

Artan, Tülay (1989) *Architecture as a Theatre of Life: Profile of the Eighteenth-Century Bosphorus.* Unpublished dissertation, MIT.

Aslan, Rıfkı (1989). "Gecekondulaşmanın Evrimi." *Mimarlık* 6.

Bartu, Ayfer (2000). "Kentsel Ayrı(şı)m: İstanbul'daki Yeni, Yerleşimler ve Kemer Country Örneği." In F. Gümüşoğlu (ed.) *21. Yüzyılda Kent ve İnsan.* İstanbul: Bağlam Yayınları.

Batur, Afife (1984). "To Be Modern: Search for a Republican Architecture." In R. Holod and A. Evin (eds.) *Modern Turkish Architecture.* Philadelphia: University of Pennsylvania Press, pp. 68–93.

Beaverstock, J. V., R.G. Smith and P. J. Taylor (1999). "A Roster of World Cities." *Cities* 16 (6), pp. 445–458.

Bilgin, İhsan (1998). "Modernleşme ve Toplumsal Hareketliliğin Yörüngesinde Cumhuriyet'in İmarı." *75 Yılda Değişen Kent ve Mimarlı.* İstanbul: Tarih Vakfi Yayınları, pp. 255–272.

Blakely, E. J. (1992). *Shaping the American Dream: Land Use Choices for America's Future.* Working Paper No. 588, Institute for Urban and Regional Development, University of California, Berkeley.

Cengiz, Hüseyin (1995). *İstanbul'un Çağdaş Metropolitan Kent Merkezi Oluşumu: Büyükdere Aksı* [The Formation of Istanbul's Contemporary City Center: Büyükdere Boulevard], Yıldız Technical University Publications, no. 95.072.

Çelik, Zeynep (1986). *The Remaking of Istanbul.* Seattle and London: University of Washington Press.

Dinçer İclal, and Zeynep Merey Enlil (2003). "Eski Kent Merkezinde Yeni Yoksullar: Tarlabaşı, İstanbul." *Yoksulluk, Kent Yoksulluğu ve Planlama,* 8 Kasım Dünya Şehircilik Günü, 26. Kollokyumu, 6-8 Kasım 2002, Ankara.

Dökmeci, Vedia, and Lale Berköz (1994). "Transformation of Istanbul from a Monocentric to Polycentric City." *European Planning Studies 2(2),* 193–205.

Ekinci, Oktay (1993). "Turizmi Teşvik Yasası ve Yağmalanan Istanbul." *Istanbul Dergisi* 6, pp. 18–23.

Enlil, Zeynep Merey (2005). "Contested Spaces at the Core and the Periphery: Fragmentation and Social Polarization in Istanbul's Residential Neighborhoods." AESOP Congress, "*Dream of a Greater Europe,*" 13–17 July 2005, Vienna, Austria.

Enlil, Zeynep Merey (2003a). "1980 Sonrası Istanbul'da Toplumsal Ayrışmanın Mekansal İzdüşümleri." *mimar.ist* 3(8), pp. 84–89.

Enlil, Zeynep Merey (2003b). "Yeni Zenginlerin Saklı Kentlerinden Yeni Yoksulların Terkedilmiş Kentlerine: 1980 Sonrası Istanbul'un Kültürel Peyzajı." In *Yoksulluk, Kent Yoksulluğu ve Planlama,* 8 Kasım Dünya Şehircilik Günü, 26. Kollokyumu, 6–8 Kasım 2002, Ankara.

Enlil, Zeynep Merey, and İclal Dinçer (2000a). "Istanbul'un Kültürel Peyzajı: Uzlaşma ve Çatışma Mekanları." *3. Bin Yılda Şehirler: Mekan, Planlama, Küreselleşme,* in İ. Dinçer (ed.) Dünya Şehircilik Günü 23. Kolokyumu, 8–10 Kasım 1999, YTÜ, İstanbul, pp. 203–210.

Enlil, Zeynep Merey (2000b). "Yeniden İşlevlendirme ve Soylulaştırma: Bir Sınıfsal Proje Olarak Eski Kent Merkezlerinin ve Tarihi Konut DokusununYeniden Ele Geçirilmesi." *domus m*, Aralık no. 8, pp. 46–49.

Enlil, Zeynep Merey, Zekai Görgülü, and İclal Dinçer (1998). "Management and Mismanagement of Change in the 'Grand Water Allée:' The Case of the Bosphorus." *Land and Water: Integrated Planning for a Sustainable Future,* 34th International Planning Congress-ISoCaRP, 26 September–2 October 1998, Azores, Portugal; *Land and Water: Integrated Planning for a Sustainable Future—Working Paper Book,* pp. 257–262.

Enlil, Zeynep Merey, (1994b) "From Traditional House to Apartment House: Seventy Years of Transformation in Istanbul's Nineteenth-Century Neighborhoods—The Case of Ni anta ı." In "*Planning for a Broader Europe,*" VIII AESOP Congress, 24–27 August 1994, Istanbul, Proceedings, vol. 4. pp. 76–99. Istanbul: YTU-Faculty of Architecture Press.

Enlil, Zeynep Merey (1994a). *Continuity and Change in Istanbul's Nineteenth- Century Neighborhoods: From Traditional House to Apartment House.* Unpublished dissertation, University of Washington, Seattle.

Erder, Sema (1996). *İstanbul'a Bir Kent Kondu: Ümraniye.* İstanbul: İletişim Yayınları.

Friedmann, J. (1986). "The World City Hypothesis." *Development and Change,* vol.17, pp. 69–83.

Güvenç, Murat (2000). "İstanbul'u Haritalamak: 1990 Sayımından İstanbul Manzaraları." *Istanbul,* no. 34, pp. 35–40.

Güvenç, Murat (1993). "Metropol Değil Azman Sanayi Kenti." *Istanbul,* no. 5, pp. 75–81.

Hall, Peter (1984). *The World Cities,* 3d ed. London: Weidenfeld and Nicolson.

Hall, Tim (1998). *Urban Geograph.* London and New York: Routledge.

Islam, Tolga, and Zeynep Merey Enlil (2006). "Evaluating the Impact of Gentrification on Renter Local Residents: The Dynamics of Displacement in Galata, Istanbul, 42 Planning Congress of ISoCaRP, "*Cities between Integration and Disintegration: Challenges and Opportunities,*" 14–18 September 2006, Istanbul.

Islam, Tolga (2005). "Outside the Core: Gentrification in Istanbul." In R. Atkinson and G. Bridges (eds.) *The New Urban Colonialism: Gentrification in a Global Context.* London and New York: Routledge, pp. 121–136.

Işık, Oğuz, and Melih Pınarcıoğlu (2001). *Nöbetleşe Yoksulluk: Sultanbeyli Örneği,* İstanbul: İletişim Yayınları.

Kaptan, Hüseyin (1991). "*The Development Process of the Service Sector in the Istanbul Metropolitan Area: An Analysis of the Büyükdere Sub-region.*" Unpublished research report.

Kaptan, Hüseyin (1991). "Changing Face of Istanbul Metropolitan Area within the Context of Tourism." In Z. Yenen (ed.) *International Symposium on the Architecture of Tourism in the Mediterranean,* Proceedings, vol. 1, pp. 51–71.

Kaptan, Hüseyin (1989). "Directions of Urban Formation in İstanbul Metropolitan Areas as Time Goes By," *Metropolitan Development in an Industrializing Country: The Case of Metropoltan Istanbul.* Paper submitted to the Nineteenth International Fellows Conference, METU and Johns Hopkins University, Istanbul, 17–23 June 1989.

Kaptan, Hüseyin (1988). *Metropolitan Alan İçinde Düşük Gelir Grubunun Yerleşme Düzeni.* İstanbul: Yildiz Universitesi, Mimarlık Fakultesi, Şehir ve Bolge Planlama Bolumu.

Kaptan, Hüseyin (1988). *E-5 Koridoru Harem-Gebze Nazım Imar Planı Raporu*. Istanbul.

Keyder, Çağlar, and Ayşe Öncü (1994). "Globalization of a Third World Metropolis: Istanbul in the 1980s," *Review*, 17(3), pp. 383–421.

Keyder, Çağlar, and Ayşe Öncü (1993). "Istanbul Yol Ayrımında." *Istanbul Dergisi*, no. 7, pp. 28–35.

Kurtuluş, Hatice (2005). "İstanbul'da Kapalı Yerleşmeler: Beykoz Konakları Örneği." In H. Kurtuluş (ed.) *İstanbul'da Kentsel Ayrışma*. Ankara: Bağlam Yayıncılık, pp. 161–186.

Kurtuluş, Hatice (2005). "Bir 'Utopya' Olarak Bahçeşehir." In H. Kurtuluş (ed.) *İstanbul'da Kentsel Ayrışma*. Ankara: Bağlam Yayıncılık, pp. 77–126.

Ley, David (1994). "Gentrification and the Politics of New Middle Class." *Environment and Planning D: Society and Space*, 12, 57.

Lewis, Bernard (1969). *The Emergence of Modern Turkey*, 2d ed. Oxford and London: Oxford University Press.

Marcuse, Peter (1993). "What's So New About Divided Cities?" *IJJUR*, 17(3), pp. 355–365.

Marcuse, Peter, and Ronald van Kempen, eds. (1999). *Globalizing Cities: Is There a New Spatial Order?* Oxford: Blackwell.

Mingione, Enzo (ed.) (1996). *Urban Poverty and the Underclass*. Oxford: Blackwell.

Özdemir, Dilek (2002). "The Distibution of Foreign Direct Investment in the Service Sector in Istanbul." *Cities*, 19(4), pp. 249–259.

Özdemir, Dilek (2000). "Yabancı Sermayenin İstanbul Haritası." *İstanbul*, Sayı 35, 96–104.

Öncü, Ay e (1997) "The Myth of the 'Ideal Home' Travels across Cultural Borders to İstanbul." In A. Öncü and P. Weyland (eds.) *Space, Culture, and Power: New Identities in Globalizing Cities*. London and New Jersey: Zed Books, pp. 56–72.

Öncü, Ayşe (1988). "The Politics of Urban Land Market in Turkey: 1950–1980." *IJURR*, 12(1), pp. 38–63.

Sassen, Sasskia (2002). "Locating Cities on Global Circuits." *Environment & Urbanization* 14(1), April, pp. 13–30.

Sassen, Sasskia (1995). "Urban Impacts of Economic Globalization." In J. Brotchie, M. Batty, E. Blakely, P. Hall, and P. Newton (eds.) *Cities in Competition*. Australia: Longman, pp. 36–57.

Sassen, Sasskia (1994). *Cities in a World Economy*. Thousand Oaks, CA: Pine Forge-Sage.

Sassen, Sasskia (1991). *Global City: London, New York, Tokyo*. Princeton: Princeton University Press.

Shaw, Stanford, J. (1979). "The Population of Istanbul in the Nineteenth Century." *International Journal of Middle East Studies* (10), pp. 265–277.

Smith, N. (1987). "Gentrification and the Rent-Gap." *Annals of the Association of American Geographers* 77 (3), pp. 462–465.

Swyngedouw, Erik, Frank Moulaert, and Arantxa Rodriguez (2002). "Neoliberal Urbanization in Europe: Large-Scale Urban Development Projects and the New Urban Policy." *Antipode*, vol. 32, pp. 542–577.

Şengezer, Betül Sayın, and Zeynep Merey Enlil (1999). "Opportunities Provided by the Transformation of Industrial Areas: Towards Sustainable Development in the İstanbul Metropolitan Region." In *The Future of Industrial Regions: Regional Strategies and Local Action Towards Sustainability—Working Paper Book*. 35th International Planning Congress-ISoCaRP, 17–20 September 1999, Gelsenkirchen, Germany, pp. 246–250.

Tekeli, İlhan (2001). *Modernite Aşılırken Kent Planlaması*. İmge Kitapevi Yayınları: Istanbul.

Tekeli, İlhan (1992a). "Development of Urban Administration and Planning in the Formation of Istanbul Metropolitan Area." In İ. Tekeli, T. Şenyapılı, A. Türel, M. Güvenç, and E. Acar. *Development of İstanbul Metropolitan Area and Low- Cost Housing*. Turkish Social Science Association, Municipality of Greater Istanbul, IULA-EMME, Istanbul.

Tekeli, İlhan (1992b). "Yüzelli Yılda Toplu Ulaşım." *Istanbul Dergisi*, no. 2, pp. 18–27.

Tekeli, İlhan, and Selim İlkin (n.d.). "1923 Yılında Istanbul'un Iktisadi Durumu ve Istanbul Ticaret Odası Komisyonu Raporu." *Istanbul Konferansları*, pp. 271–272.

Tercan, Binali (1996). "Günümüze Değin İmar Afları." *Planlama* no. 1–4, pp. 5–8.

Tokatlı, Nebahat, and Yonca Boyacı (1999). "The Changing Morphology of Commercial Activity in Istanbul." *Cities*, 16(3), pp. 181–193.

Türksoy, Cengiz (1996). "İmar Af mı?" *Planlama* no. 1–4, pp. 9–14.

Uzun, Nil C. (2001). *Gentrification in Istanbul: A Diagnostic Study*." Nederlandse Geografische Studies 285, Utrecht.

Wolf, Martin (2005). "Turkey—Rising Star?" ULI
Conference on "*Emerging European Real
Estate Markets: Trends, Challenge,s and
Opportunities.*" 1–2 June 2005, Istanbul.

Yenen, Zekiye, Zeynep Merey Enlil, and Yalçın
Ünal (1993) "İstanbul: A City of Waterfronts
or a City Inland." In R. Brutomesso (ed.)
*Waterfronts: A New Frontier for Cities on
Water.* Venice: Rizzoli, pp. 116–123.

Notes

1. According to a study done by Beaverstock
   et al. (1999), Istanbul ranks as a third-tier or
   "gamma" city in the world hierarchy due to
   a major concentration of international
   firms in advertising and a minor concentration of banking and legal services.
2. For a discussion of new underclass, see, for
   instance, E. Mingione (ed.) 1996.
3. For a full overview of the nineteenth-century changes in the city, see Z. Çelik (1986).
4. The rate of decrease was most significant
   among the Greek community. Istanbul was
   not only reduced in size but became demo-
   graphically more homogenized. According
   to the 1885 census, Muslims comprised 44
   percent of the population, non-Muslims 41
   percent, Europeans and foreign passport
   holders, 15 percent (Shaw 1979, p. 268). By
   1927, Muslims made up 64 percent, non-
   Muslims 27 percent, and foreigners 9 percent of the city's population (Tekeli 1992a,
   p. 21).
5. See Tekeli and Ilkin (n.d.) for a report prepared by the Economic Commission of
   Istanbul Chamber of Commerce on the
   Economic Conditions of Istanbul in 1923,
   pp. 271–272.
6. For a full discussion of the Prost Plan and
   its execution under the administration of
   Lütfi Kırdar, governor and mayor of
   Istanbul, see Tekeli 1992a, pp. 29–40.
7. Wartime brought high demand for Turkish
   agricultural products and boosted Turkish
   foreign trade. This development, coupled
   with the high rate of governmental military spending, caused severe shortages of
   essential commodities in the domestic
   market and increased inflationary pressures. Two groups profited from these conditions. First, farmers with large land
   holdings benefited from the high demand
   and rise in price of their products. Second,
   the merchants and intermediaries of
   Istanbul found favorable conditions to
   exploit both the high value of Turkish

   exports and the acute shortage of essential imports. Once again, the end of the
   war found Turkey with a new class of rich
   men (B. Lewis 1969, p. 473).
8. For a study on the residential patterns of
   Muslims and non-Muslims, and the elite
   and non-elite, and how they mixed along
   the eighteenth-century Bosphorus, see
   Artan 1989; for a discussion of how these
   patterns changed as a result of nineteenth-century transformations, see Enlil
   1994a.
9. For a study of the transformation of housing patterns in the prestigious neighborhood of Nişantaşı, see Enlil 1994b.
10. Between 1960 and 1964, 80 percent of the
    foreign capital flowing into the country
    chose Istanbul as the main area of invest-
    ment. For a concise overview of industrial
    development in Istanbul, see Istanbul
    Ansiklopedisi, pp. 437–443.
11. In 1950 there were 15,342 small-scale
    establishments with fewer than ten
    employees and 610 establishments with
    more than ten employees in Istanbul.
    According to the 1964 census of industry
    and business firms, these figures went up
    to 30,579 and 1,293 respectively. The share
    of Istanbul within the country, however,
    did not change much, as the former consti-
    tuted 18 percent of the total in both 1950
    and 1964; and the latter rose from 40 per-
    cent of the total in 1950 to 42 percent in
    1964 (Tekeli, p. 55).
12. For a full overview of the period, see
    Istanbul Ansiklopedisi, pp. 442–443.
13. The 40-kilometer distance on the Anatolian
    side is defined by the administrative
    boundaries of the Municipality of Greater
    Istanbul, which has recently been extend-
    ed to overlap with the boundaries of the
    Province of Istanbul, to include the enor-
    mous sprawl under one administrative
    area. The extent of the Istanbul
    Metropolitan Area, however, is not actually
    limited by its administrative boundaries;
    right outside its boundary on the east
    extends a wide stretch of an intensely
    industrialized area in the Municipality of
    Gebze. Even though Gebze is within the
    administrative boundaries of the Province
    of Kocaeli, it is organically linked to
    Istanbul and constitutes the eastern wing
    of the Istanbul Metropolitan Area.
14. The number of vehicles crossing the
    Bosphorus daily in 1972, before the first

bridge over the Bosphorus was constructed, was 16,000; in 1975, two years after the bridge was put into service, the number increased to 56,000. Of these 51,500 were via the bridge, with only 3,700 via ferries. The number of passengers crossing the Bosphorus daily, on the other hand, was 337,000 in 1972 and increased only to 384,000 by 1975. Of these crossings, 279,000 were still made by ferries, whereas 91,000 passengers crossed the bridge by private car and 14,000 by public buses (Tekeli 1992b). The number of vehicles passing over the two bridges increased by 21 times by 1994, whereas the number of passengers increased only 4 times.

15. The first law to grant amnesty to illegal developments was passed in 1948, limited to the *gecekondus* in Ankara. The law stipulated the transfer of the lands belonging to the Treasury occupied by *gecekondus* to the municipalities, to be then sold to the inhabitants of these illegal settlements. Another law in 1949 extended the amnesty to the rest of the country. See Enlil and Dincer (1999).

16. In this form of land provision, also translated as "shared title," people owned a certain percentage of a large tract of subdivided land, which did not involve a legally defined unit or a lot corresponding to a certain spatial location.

17. For a full discussion of the policy packages and their ramifications, see Keyder and Öncü (1994), pp. 400–405, and Kaptan (1991), pp. 12–16.

18. Although producer services grew rapidly, their share within total emplyment was rather low: they accounted for 5.29 percent of total employment in 1980, 7.07 percent in 1990, and 8.16 percent in 2000. The share of producer services within total employment in the services sector was 10.3 percent in 1980 and 13.9 percent in 1990, while it increased to 15.3 percent by 2000. For 1980 and 1990 figures, see Aksoy 1996, pp. 24 and 33; for 2000 figures, see DIE 2000, Population Census, pp. 202–203.

19. According to Berköz, total foreign capital investment in Turkey was $655,240,000 in 1987. By 1997 this figure had risen to $1,645,760,000. In 1987 there were only 795 foreign firms in Turkey, while their number reached 3,707 by 1997. Of these, 963 were in manufacturing, 98 in agriculture, and 2,646 in services (in 1987, however, the figures for

manufacturing, agriculture, and service sectors were 255, 35, and 505 respectively). See Berköz 2000, p. 76.

20. For a full account of these transformations, see H. Cengiz 1995, D. Özdemir 2000 and 2002, and V. Dökmeci and L. Berköz 1994.

21. For a full discussion of the clearing of industry, see Kaptan 1991, pp. 10–12.

22. The only exception was Migros-Turk supermarket, which remained as the unique example until the withdrawal of the Swiss Federation from the Turkish market in 1975 (Tokatlı and Boyacı 1999, p. 187).

23. For a detailed analysis of the spatial distribution of population groups along various parameters, see M. Güvenç (2000).

24. Another reason for this fall was the shift of small capital from housing production to more profitable channels of accumulation such as increased interest rates and the foundation of the Istanbul Stock Exchange; see Bilgin (1998).

25. ANAP intervened in the housing market because the construction sector generated activity in other sectors, boosting the economy.

26. Initially, the production by these cooperatives worked in a similar way to that of the *yap-sat* model; the enlargement of the scale of production did not necessarily mean the modernization of the organization of production, usage of modern building construction technology, and rigorous advertising and marketing strategies (Bilgin 1998, p. 267).

27. The production of mass housing by a corporation of Greater Istanbul Municipality, KIPTAŞ, is also worth mentioning. Established in 1987 and restructured to function efficiently in 1995, KIPTAŞ has been a significant actor in the housing sector with an aim to provide affordable housing and a solution to illegal, unhealthy developments. With the motto of "50,000 units for Istanbul," it produced, since 1995, 20,322 units on the European Side and 5,555 units on the Anatolian side of the city, again built as high-rise apartment complexes on the periphery; see www.kiptas.com.tr. Kiptaş has been influential in transforming the urban form of Istanbul by building in large fragments.

28. We borrow this conceptualization of the city divided into fragments from

P. Marcuse (1993). Through his analysis of New York City, Marcuse contends that the contemporary city can be seen as divided roughly into five segments. His categories include: "luxury housing," the enclaves of the top economic, social, and political elite; "the gentrified city" of the professional, managerial, and technical groups without children; "the suburban city" of the skilled workers and mid-level professionals and civil servants; "the tenement city" of the lower-paid blue- and white-collar workers and social housing dwellers; the "abandoned city" of the poor, the unemployed, and the excluded and of the informal economy. Istanbul's experience has its own peculiarities. It is somewhat similar but does not correspond exactly with the experience of its counterparts in the advanced economies of the West. The main differences concern suburban and tenement cities as described by Marcuse and the Turkish case. For a more detailed reading of Istanbul through the same lens, see Enlil (2003a) and (2003b).

29. For an extensive analysis of the Amnesty Laws, see Tercan (1996) and Türksoy (1996).

30. Keyder and Öncü (1994) argue that "de-regulation of the residential property market promised instant gains to those whose real income deteriorated under the austerity measures and compensated for the decline in real wages, rising unemployment and polarizing income distribution" (p. 399). For a full review of how the rural migrants seized urban rents as a way out of poverty, see Işık and Pınarcıoğlu (2001). For a similar study, also see Erder (1996).

31. Among the growing amount of literature on gated communities in Istanbul, see Öncü (1997), and Enlil (2003a) and (2003b); for detailed studies on settlements such as Kemer Country, see Bartu (2000); on Beykoz Konakları, see Kurtulus (2005).

32. Some early examples include Platin Residences on the European side and Avrupa Konakları on the Anatolian side.

33. These aspects are stressed in the marketing campaigns for these residential developments and are mentioned by their residents in magazine interviews. Yet also emphasized is quick accessibility to Maslak, the new central business district, via new roads and viaducts. See Enlil (2003a).

34. Used here in the sense of Bourdieu (1984).

35. For a discussion of how the middle classes emulated the patterns of the new elite, see Öncü (1997).

36. The incidents of 6–7 September and the Cyprus crises brought about hostility toward the non-Muslim population of the city. The areas most affected by this turmoil were neighborhoods such as Fener and Balat in the Istanbul Peninsula and Galata and Beyoğlu. The conflicts resulted in the exodus of the remnants of the minorities from the country.

37. Overcrowding is a common feature of these quarters, where two families share a small building built as a single-family home in the nineteenth century.

38. For a full review of how the rural migrants seized urban rents as a way out of poverty, see Işık and Pınarcıoğlu (2001). For a similar study, also see Erder (1996). These success stories should not be taken to mean that poverty does not exist on the periphery. The living conditions of migrants in these informal settlements have always been much worse than in the formal sections of the city.

39. This was a more prominent characteristic of later generations of migrants. The majority were from the poorest eastern and southeastern regions of the country and arrived in the city since the second part of the 1980s and into the 1990s.

40. The master plan approved in 1980 proposed the decentralization of large-scale and polluting industry, and new industrial zones were established on the outskirts of the city. Later on, large-scale plants were encouraged to move further out to the new industrial zone in Çorlu in the province of Tekirdağ, to the west of the province of Istanbul.

41. Those who were born in Istanbul were second- or third-generation migrants. The rate of unemployment among them was 35 percent, while it was only 9 percent among those who came to the city before 1990s and 12 percent for the newcomers after the 1990s. Only 17 percent of those who were born in Istanbul were homeowners in the neighborhood, whereas this ratio was 46 percent and 12 percent for those who came before and after the 1990s, respectively. For a detailed analysis along various other parameters, see Dinçer and Enlil (2003).

42. Added to this scene in Tarlabaşı are the elderly, transvestites, and a new group of international migrants mostly from Africa ("Afro-Istanbulites" as one journalist called them). See Sarıbaş, Şermin, *Hürriyet,* Pazar Eki, 17 Haziran 2001.

43. For a detailed study of gentrification in Kuzguncuk and Cihangir, see Uzun (2001).

44. In the 1960s and 1970s the district was marked by cheap nightclubs and illicit activities, from prostitution to drug trafficking. Its once fashionable movie theaters became places for low-budget and sometimes pornographic domestic films.

45. Ley defines these classes as tertiary educated groups in the arts, media, teaching, and academic positions as well as public sector managers in regulatory and welfare activities. See D. Ley (1994), p. 56.

46. For a study of the gentrification process in Galata, see T. Islam (2005).

47. N. Smith defines rent gap as the disparity between "the actual capitalized ground rent (land value) of a plot of land given its present use and the potential ground rent that might be gained under a higher and better use" (1987), p. 462.

48. According to the chief economic commentator of the *Financial Times,* Martin Wolf, Turkey is a rising star. Another commentator called Istanbul "the hottest destination for property investors in Turkey." See Wolf (2005) and www.shelteroffshore.com. For issues related to rising real estate values in Istanbul, see ULI Conference *on "Developing Markets in Central and Eastern Europe,"* 1–3 May 2005, Istanbul, *Arkitera,* 18 May 2005.

MURAT GUVENC

ANKARA

FROM A STRUCTURALLY
CONTAINED TO A SPRAWLING
CAPITAL CITY

In this chapter, I attempt to describe the emergence of the urban
macro form of Ankara as a unique event in the history of urbanization
in Turkey. The discussion is presented in two sections. The first provides a brief overview of Turkish demography and urban history; the
second concentrates on the emergence of the current macro form of
Ankara. In the second part the emphasis will be on local geographic
features, patterns of social geography, intra-urban mobility, and land
ownership. This dual perspective aims to illustrate not only the
processes that led to the emergence of the city's macro form but also
the differences and similarities of Ankara with respect to Istanbul
and Izmir, the two other vertices of the Turkish triangle.

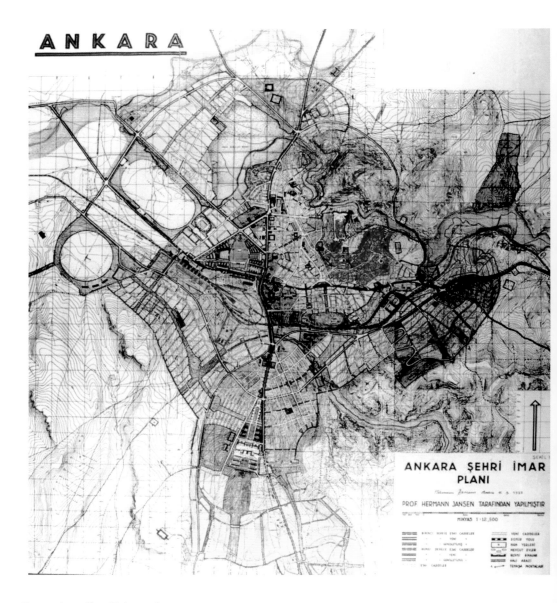

Hermann Jansen Plan of Ankara, 1928.

TURKEY'S URBANIZATION HISTORY: AN OVERVIEW

It is convenient to study Turkey's modernization history as three periods of approximately twenty-five years each, with distinctive regimes of accumulation, modalities of global economic integration, modes of social regulation, and types of governance. This swift process transformed what was a predominantly agricultural country into a largely industrial and service economy. The first period started with the proclamation of the Republic in 1923 and extended to 1946, the date of the first multiparty election in Turkey; this is usually referred to as an era of radical modernity. The second phase, beginning in 1946 and ending with the military coup d'état in 1980, is often called a period of populist modernity. The third period, from 1980 to the present, distinguishes itself by the gradual dismantling of production systems and modes of governance set up during the import-substitution period of a rising market economy, the devolution of power to local authorities, and the advent of customs union and increased integration with the European Union and the global economy.

In a seminal historical overview of Turkey's urbanization, Ilhan Tekeli convincingly illustrates that each of these periods corresponds to a different phase in Turkish urbanization, with distinctive urban processes, modes of housing supply, organization of intra-urban transport, intra-urban distribution of workplaces and residences, and urban governance.[1]

During the three decades that followed the proclamation of the Republic, Turkey remained a predominantly rural country, with only a gradual annual increase in the rate of urban population growth. Ankara, the new capital, did experience rapid growth. The second phase of Turkey's urbanization started with the end of World War II and ended with a series of petroleum shocks, which through their impact on the balance of payments threatened the import-substitution strategy. During this period of sustained economic growth (1945–75), Turkey faced rapid urban growth that was not associated with urban decentralization and suburbanization.

The macroeconomic policy of import substitution reduced substantially the funds available for public investments and mortgage systems that would support urban decentralization. Major cities were unable to produce land and experienced density increases. This rapid urban growth took a heavy toll on civilian architecture and had negative effects on the quality of urban life, including the provision of public services. Metropolises were surrounded by a belt of squatter settlements; shared taxis emerged as an ad hoc solution to a growing transport problem and generated a substantial informal economy (though not enough purchasing power to support subcenters in squatter areas). Tekeli et al.'s *City of Squatters, Shared Taxis, and Street Vendors* is a succinct account of the emergence of spatial organization, transport, physical planning, and governance difficulties.[2]

After the global crisis of 1973, this regime proved unsustainable and there was a painful reversal in Turkey's macroeconomic policies, with a gradual transition from import substitution to a more liberal regime and greater integration with the world economy. This third phase is associated with a comprehensive privatization project, dismantling of state-run economic enterprises, erosion of the bargaining power of trade unions, liberalization of foreign trade, and enhanced integration with the world economy, all of which had non-negligible impacts on urban processes. Governments that took office in this third phase were gradually freed from their role as direct investors in manufacturing and as regulators and guarantors of minimum prices for agricultural produce. The removal of government's responsibility for manufacturing and service provision created opportunities to make up for inadequate investments in transport and telecommunications, highways, electrification, airports, and other urban infrastructure. The relaxation of strict planning controls, the establishment of new housing credit programs, and the devolution of power to local authorities provided a favorable context for fringe developments and urban sprawl.

It follows that cities confined to compact macro forms in the previous period, where the requirement for development land was highest, started to decentralize in the third phase to compensate for the underconsumption of space that characterized previous decades. Hence cities in Turkey confined to compact macro forms started to decentralize by the 1980s, when population pressure and the demand for development land was significantly less. A major part of Ankara's current macro form was shaped in this third period.

TURKEY'S DEMOGRAPHY

These policies were associated with significant changes in the national distribution of population. These three phases of Turkey's urbanization are linked with two distinctive phases in demographic trends. In the first phase, a time of practically no migration, the population pyramid reflected the effects of wars. High mortality and fertility rates had shaped an age distribution characteristic of agrarian economies. After World War II, the mechanization of agriculture gave impetus to urbanization. This second period distinguishes itself with declining mortality, but a relatively high, stable fertility rate and high rural-to-urban migration. In spite of the high rate of urbanization, however, the age pyramid for 1960 was not significantly different than that drawn for 1935. The third phase distinguishes itself by decreasing fertility, new migration flow patterns, increasing life expectancy, significant increases in the median age of marriage, an overall flattening of the age-specific fertility curve, and improvements in women's education and in infant and child mortality. The age pyramid for 1990 depicts a stabilization of the first three cohorts, and the transition to a stable population is expected to be complete in 2050. The latest nationwide survey suggests that the process of demographic transition is happening faster than anticipated. Rapidly industrializing Western Turkey, a major hub of economic activity and a beneficiary of the modernization process, increased its population share from 28 percent to 38 percent within forty-five years.

Despite significant regional variations, the total fertility rate reflects significant decreases. As was the case in most developing countries, urbanization went hand in hand with a swift decrease in infant and child mortality, and slower decreases in total

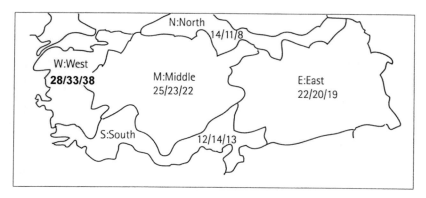

Population shares accounted for by the demographic regions
of the State Institute of Statistics (share 1960/share
1990/share 2003). Source: State Institute of Statistics.

fertility rates. The gradual adoption of urban ways of life, availability of new medical technology, and improvements in women's education affected the median age of marriage and childbearing, infant mortality, and life expectancy.

The evolution of the three major demographic components suggests that the first two phases of Republican history were periods of rapid population growth and that the third period, started in 1980 and characterized by a stabilization of the "young," emerged as a window of opportunity for attracting foreign direct investment and improving the quality of public services. Demographic transition is of course a long and a slow process. Yet what took Europe two centuries to complete will be accomplished in Turkey's case in less than one.

CHANGES IN THE NATIONAL ECONOMIC LANDSCAPE

The three metropolises of the Turkish Triangle are the three largest cities of Turkey. That their scale brings qualitative differences in lifestyle is undeniable. An overemphasis on their shared scale and lifestyle, however, hides important differences among them. Located in different regional settings, the three major cities have inherently different natural endowments and are specialized in different economic sectors.

Based on employment figures in major sectors of economic activity for 1990 and 2000, Turkey's provinces fall into three major constellations. Provinces with significant agricultural employment constitute the first, and manufacturing employment the second constellation. Ankara, with a significant overrepresentation of jobs in social and public services, emerges as the third element of the economic landscape. The three vertices of the Turkish Triangle are major centers of activity in this spatial organization. Istanbul ranks first in terms of population, but is the smallest of the three provinces. Situated on a narrow peninsula, the city had a chronic inability to feed itself. But the city distinguishes itself as a manufacturing and international trade center. Endowed with none of the climatic advantages of Istanbul and Izmir, Ankara is important in cereal production only. The province of Ankara, where capital-intensive dry farming is dominant, is far from the province of Izmir, which is specialized in relatively labor-intensive Mediterranean crops such as tobacco, grapes, and olives.

As a consequence of deindustrialization and the rise of a service economy, Istanbul shifted away from manufacturing and toward transport, communications, and services. Izmir, a gateway to one of the richest agricultural regions, is deepening its specialization in retail and wholesale trade transport and communications and producer services. Ankara, unaffected by these processes, continues to specialize in administrative services. In spite of its formidable growth during the first two periods, Ankara did not specialize in areas of activity that would allow it to compete with Istanbul and Izmir. Comparisons that are not attentive to these contextual differences cannot convey a relevant account of the situation.

In the early 1930s, the context was totally different. Istanbul and Izmir were stagnating cities whereas Ankara, despite its evident situational disadvantage, emerged as a major growth area. During the three decades following its proclamation as the capital, the annual population growth rate was on the order of 5.5 percent, while Istanbul and Izmir stagnated. Izmir, the second-largest port, was war stricken, had a great fire, and had lost a major part of its economically active population in the population transfer between Greece and Turkey. Last but not least, the new étatist economic policies and the falling prices of agricultural produce impeded its development during the Great Depression. The fate of Istanbul was no better. As a result of the nationalization of railroad, tramway, gas, electricity, and water companies, and of the lucrative tobacco industry, the city ceased to be a hub of economic activity and center of diplomacy. In 1927, Istanbul's population was down to 0.7 million from 1.4 million in 1914. In the transfer of capital city functions to Ankara, the city lost thousands of secure and relatively well-paying jobs, and its diplomatic corps.

For Ankara, on the other hand, the 1930s were golden years. Thanks to its central position in the emerging nation-state, it was the headquarters of the Turkish war of independence and seat of the first national assembly; it was proclaimed the capital of the Turkish Republic in 1923. Its obvious situational advantages and its rapid development of a service economy had sustained population growth and made it emerge as the second-largest city of Turkey.

Mechanization of Turkey's agriculture gained impetus with the U.S. Marshall Plan after World War II. Unprecedented population growth and its self-propelling urban dynamics were to a large extent unanticipated, but fueled the process of integration of national markets. Thus rapid population growth that was unique to Ankara was transformed into a more generalized phenomenon.

A visitor to today's Ankara would hardly believe that this large agglomeration of 3.6 million had a population of only 75,000 in 1927 and about half that size prior to the proclamation of the Republic; it doubled its population every ten years.

The urban population of Ankara doubled between 1927 and 1940, and tripled between 1927 and 1950. The city's population rose from 650,000 in 1960 to 1.7 million in 1975, and to 1.9 million in 1980.[3] This explosive population growth slowed down after the 1980s. Even the most experienced planners could not have accurately predicted such phenomenal growth of a remote minor provincial trading town, a terminal on the Anatolian railway, into a metropolitan area of 3.6 million.

As a result, Ankara's history and urban fabric are shaped by a succession of partially implemented, revised, and amended plans and building regulations. Although the same procedures are applied in all cities, Ankara distinguishes itself by significantly higher levels of success in plan implementation. The city experienced three major planning interventions in its urban development. The first two underestimated population growth, whereas the third slightly overestimated the growth of the urban population.

During the first period, Ankara enjoyed its status as a favored city. Many public buildings, a number of major axes, the street layout of the New Town, and recreation facilities (the Youth and Kurtulus parks realized according to the Jansen Plan adopted in 1932 are preserved.

Unfortunately, most of the private housing stock constructed in the first two decades, including the first Garden City initiative, was destroyed and replaced by apartment blocs in the second wave of contiguous urban growth.

The city in the 1930s must have looked like an island of modernity in the middle of the backward central Anatolian Plateau, where there was high illiteracy, fertility, and infant and adult mortality rates. Life expectancy was as low as forty years, and there was a sharp contrast between the social and spatial structures of the city and the settlements in its immediate vicinity. The village of Balgat, only 8 kilometers from the city, was studied by Daniel Lerner. The following quotation from an informant succinctly illustrates the contrast between the city and adjacent settlements:

> I have seen quite a lot of villages in the barren mountainous East, but never such a colorless, shapeless dump. . . . It could have been half an hour to Ankara by car if it had a road, yet it is about two hours to the capital by car without almost any road and is just forgotten, forsaken, right under our noses.[4]

Transition to a multiparty system abruptly ended Ankara's golden years, and the sharp contrast started to disappear. Yet the city continued to be a destination for migrants from eastern and central Anatolia. This had important repercussions on urban morphology and social geography. In the context of new political priorities and economic policies, investment funds for urban infrastructure were significantly reduced. The scarcity of development land with adequate urban infrastructure increased land prices. The isolated implementations of the Jansen Plan were encircled by a thick belt of squat-

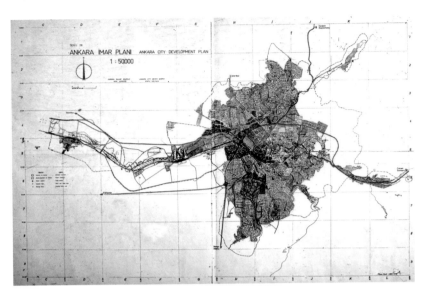

Ankara Development Plan by Yucel Uybadin, 1957.

ter housing. The donut-shaped Ankara macro form proposed by the Yücel Uybadin Plan, the winner of the planning contest of 1957, did not bring radical changes to the urban layout. The contiguous growth and infilling generated an urban morphology with four components. At the center was the government city; early migrants constituted the pedestrian city around the citadel. The government quarter of the Jansen Plan was transformed into a low-density city center. Former residences in and around the center could not compete with rising rents and were replaced by commercial establishments.

The center was surrounded by housing areas where apartment blocs replaced low-density individual houses built in the 1930s and 1940s; the apartments had significantly better urban services and were considered better places for raising children. Beyond this sector extended the squatter settlements that constituted the "other" Ankara. Despite the hollow city center, rents were high. The well-to-do, who owned property, could protect themselves against rising land prices. A majority of the middle-income groups were hit hard by rising land prices and high rents of the inner city. As opposed to the British case, there were no new towns to alleviate the adverse redistributive effect of this strict urban containment policy.[5]

Hence the donut-shaped city was a rent trap for a majority of middle-class households, who could not endure the hardships of the squatter areas yet could not transition to homeownership. They were obliged to pay more than half of their income for rents. Mobility from squatters' settlements to regular housing was limited to a lucky few.[6]

Difficulties in meeting the rising middle-class housing demand led to the eventual adoption of new laws governing home ownership, affordable mortgage credits, and the consolidation of the petty entrepreneurial form of housing supply, along with the unfortunate destruction of entire residential sectors constructed one or two decades earlier. The new apartment blocs were affordable only to the middle classes and inaccessible to those in lower income brackets. To keep commuting distances reasonable, the population increase stemming from migration had to be accommodated in a thick belt of squatter settlements constructed on public lands adjacent to the city.

The compact urban form resulting from this containment policy brought a few advantages, such as enhanced opportunities for social contacts and a rich social and intellectual scene and a lively political environment.[7] On the whole, however, it has had negative repercussions on quality of life; besides its inequitable redistributive effects, it led to an untimely destruction of private housing stock, density increases in the inner city, proliferation of squatter settlements, rapid erosion in the quality and efficiency of urban public services, congestion, and rising air pollution levels.

But thirty years after the transition to a multiparty system, Ankara's urban problems were not significantly different from those observed in other developing cities. In this second phase, Ankara faced typical problems stemming from strict urban containment policies, yet these policies were not insurmountable obstacles. To the contrary: in the 1960s and 1970s, urban planners and municipal authorities, in spite of their limited room for maneuver, were not inactive. Thanks to the dynamism, commitment, and innovative planning and negotiating talents of the small but energetic Ankara Metropolitan Plan Bureau, many crises that might have erupted were skillfully managed. Despite budget difficulties and red tape, and in close cooperation with academicians and students of urbanism and with the Ankara Municipality, a small group of planners in the newly established AMPB could generate initiatives; engage in negotiations with landowners, industrialists, and many other stakeholders; adopt a proactive planning style; make timely interventions; earmark major zones for future housing developments; and undertake major expropriations that laid the groundwork for today's Western City (Batıkent) and New Settlements (Eryaman) projects.

The same holds true for de facto reforms undertaken by Social Democrats when they were in office in the Ankara Municipality after 1973. Subjected to the strong leadership of the central government and strict budget constraints, the Social Democrat municipality devised innovative solutions to alleviate traffic management problems and to meet demands for municipal services such as roads, water supply, sewers, and public transport. This approach, known as the "New Municipality Movement," was a source of inspiration for other cities.

Until the late 1970s, however, apart from a few exceptional projects, the structural forces of urban containment prevailed, and attempted reforms were unable to fundamentally change the layout of Ankara and improve the quality of life for its inhabitants. Air pollution exceeded international standards, especially during winter months. Water supply systems designed to meet the needs of smaller predicted populations were inadequate to meet increasing water requirements; lack of maintenance, underinvestment, and unauthorized connections led to high losses. The water supply was intermittent in summer: poorly metered, and of low quality and reliability. Sixty percent of the supplied water remained unaccounted for. The quality and reliability of public services were not necessarily higher in regular housing areas. Even neighborhoods with a high percentage of foreign diplomats were not spared intermittent water supply. A sample of drinking water extracted in 1968 from a primary school in Çankaya, 500 meters from the presidential residence, failed to meet water quality standards.[8] Most squatter dwellings had no running water indoors and had to rely on public fountains.

Thus at the end of the 1970s Ankara was a city of 1.9 million without an efficient urban transport system and unable to provide alternatives to squatters and responses to middle-income housing demand. Purchasing power in large squatter areas could sustain only small subcenters. This situation led to the proliferation of daily retailing in and around the central business district, exacerbating congestion. But all of this was to change as a result of the transition to a more liberal economic regime in 1980.

THE 1980S

In Turkey as elsewhere, the dismantling of the welfare state mechanism, disinvestment, and the gradual privatization of state economic enterprises characterized the 1980s. These developments and subsequent austerity measures had high social costs. The new economic model went hand in hand with new modes of urban governance: the introduction of a two-tiered system of metropolitan administration, the devolution of power to local authorities, the adoption or amendment of laws for planning local administration, the liberalization of urban development controls, etc. The new economic conjuncture provided funds for investments in public utilities, mass transit and communications systems, state highways, and airports, and led to the nationwide completion of village electrification and investments in urban infrastructure. Adoption of the mass housing law led to the institutionalization of mass housing as the dominant mode of housing supply.

The urban impact therefore was on the whole positive. Populist building amnesty laws, including the regularization and assignment of increased building rights to squatter zones, did not lead to unfortunate developments as in Istanbul and İzmir. The closing of the AMPB was a surprising and extremely risky administrative decision. The actors and stakeholders were committed to the implementation of the proposed scheme, and thus the closing of the planning office did not halt progress. The implementation of a plan without planners is a distinctive characteristic of Ankara's planning history.

On the other hand, decreasing fertility, increasing age of marriage, flattening of the age-specific fertility curve, and the emergence of the littoral as a favored destination alleviated the population pressure on Ankara, and many of the expected adverse effects did not materialize. The development of Ankara in the 1980s remained within the limits set up in AMPB's "1990 plan" that had been approved in 1982. The plan proposed three New Town–scale major mass housing areas.

Decentralization of the population and connection to Russian natural gas distribution systems alleviated the chronic air pollution problem. The development land already expropriated and stocked was assigned to building societies or the mass housing administration. New government buildings and new headquarters for ministries were constructed along the Eskişehir highway, as proposed in the plan. The new trans-

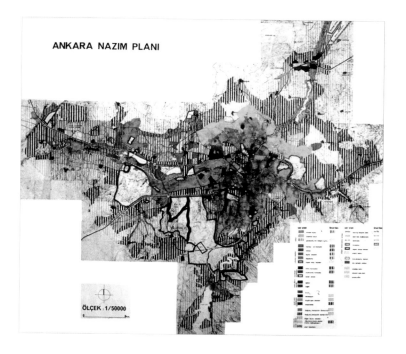

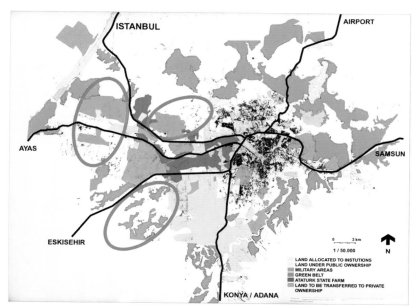

1990 Ankara Master Plan, approved in 1982.

New Town-scale major mass housing areas proposed in the 1990 Ankara Master Plan.

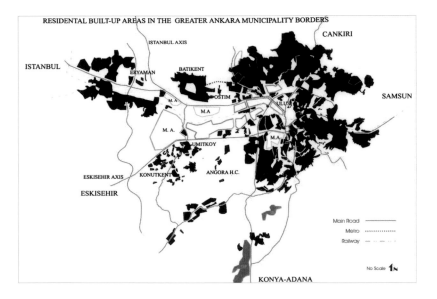

Urban growth of Ankara between 1920s and 1980s.

Built-up residential area within the Greater Ankara
Municipality borders.

port master plan adopted a scheme that was proposed in the plan. The completion of a subway connection to Batıkent fueled decentralization; 50,000 housing units were constructed within fifteen years by independent and nonprofit building societies and by the newly established mass housing administration.

The realization of major housing projects was a long-awaited development for the middle-income groups who for decades had to pay high rents in the inner city. As expected, this triggered a process of intra-urban mobility. The population increase at the inner city was practically halted, whereas metropolitan fringes experienced rapid growth. The inner-city districts account for only 11 percent and fringe districts for 89 percent of the total population increase. Differences in the rate of increase in the urban population suggest a sharper contrast: 8.4 percent for the inner city as opposed to 91.6 percent for the periphery.

A recent study on intra-metropolitan mobility suggests that the transition to home ownership emerges as a major driver in households' site selection decisions. A comparison of the social geographies of the city for 1990 and 2000 suggests continuities and ruptures. The settlement pattern is not unrelated to former social divisions. The Eryaman case aside, residents from northern sectors of the old city moved predominantly to the north and those from the south moved predominantly to southwestern Ankara. Intra-urban mobility extended but did not alleviate the sharp social contrast between northern and southern sectors of Ankara. Today Ankara has none of the problems associated to the compact and contained city of the 1970s.

The realization of the three mass housing projects at the western corridor, the subway connection to Batıkent, improvements in city buses, creation of a ring road for through traffic, and increased private car ownership made possible the decentralization of middle-class housing. Until the 1980s, practically everything was concentrated at the center. Ankara's central business district, in addition to its usual functions, had to provide a plethora of personal services and daily retailing for large residential sectors; it was an obligatory point of passage for all. The subsequent proliferation of shopping malls pushed hundreds of small retailers out of business, so that residents can now avoid the central business district for months. The low level of retail decentralization, a hallmark of the 1980s' urban macro form, has been replaced by a new retail geography. The old central business district, however, preserves its importance as a site of government jobs.

The completion of major water supply and wastewater and stormwater collection and treatment projects has reduced the vulnerability to flood risks and improved environmental quality. Rapid population and workplace decentralization and a transition to natural gas–based heating technologies significantly reduced the population pressure on environmentally sensitive topography and alleviated the city's chronic air pollution. Almost all housing units in Ankara have access to running water indoors, electricity, and drainage systems for stormwater and wastewater. A significant amount of the housing stock has access to cable television and internet connection. This constitutes a major improvement with respect to twenty years ago. Thanks to planning, and the reallocation of a vast amount of development land stock, major proposals of the metropolitan plan were realized in a liberal economic moment and without the guidance of the authors of the plan. This is a clear break, compared to the former growth pattern. By the end of the 1980s, the target year of the AMPB plan, strategic decisions of the metropolitan plan were already implemented. The current social geography of the city is an extended and slightly modified replica of the old north-south division.

LOOKING BEHIND THE MAPS: AN OVERVIEW OF THE URBAN ECOLOGY OF ANKARA

Changes in the urban macro form were in these three periods associated with significant changes in social geography. The Jansen plan's proposals pertaining to the government quarter, major schools, and public buildings were rapidly implemented, but land speculation impeded the implementation of proposals for housing in and around Yenisehir. The same held true for workers residences and the university districts invaded by squatter settlements. New housing production limited to apartment blocs around the citadel and along major arteries and single-family dwellings in and around Yenisehir could not meet the rapidly increasing demand. Scarcity of housing and development land resulted in high rents, and for decades civil servants received rent compensation payments. The first Garden City (Bahçelievler) initiative beyond the limits of the plan, and the Saracoğlu District designed by Paul Bonatz, completed in 1946, are two major projects to alleviate the housing problem of high-ranking executives.

These interventions enhanced the contrast between traditional and modern ways of life and social profiles of the old (citadel) and new (modern) Ankara. The rapid urban development in the second phase brought major changes in earlier social divisions. The traditional sectors and the citadel were physically spared from these transformations and from the negative repercussions of contiguous growth. The historical city was not particularly rich in parcels suitable for construction and service provision. Nevertheless, given its situational advantage and accessibility, the area was attractive for workers in the informal sector. This process that preserved the physical structures modified its social profile by leading to a gradual dispersal of its former residents. As a result, historical Ankara is one of the poorest sectors of the city.

Most migrants had to build individual squatter houses adjacent to the existing sectors. The situation was no better for regular housing. The early mortgage systems were inaccessible to those in need, and most potential buyers were ineligible for credit. In this context, middle- and upper-income residents relied on petty entrepreneurs, who transformed single-family residences into apartment blocs. The proliferation of squatter settlements around the citadel and at the periphery transformed the sharp contrast between the old and the new city (reflecting the incompatibility between traditional and modern modes of urban life) into a new one between the regular and irregular sectors of Ankara. The former was associated with stable formal jobs and governance systems, with comparatively higher levels of services, while the latter included the city of squatters, with informal jobs and poor services.

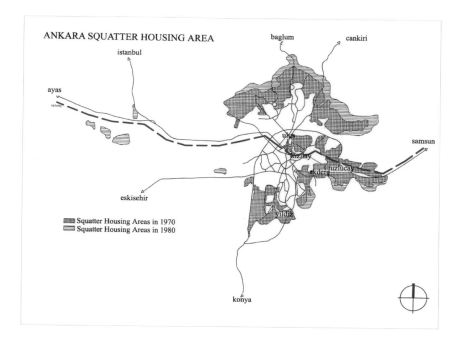

Ankara squatter housing area. Source: Ankara Master Plan Scheme report: 1970–1990.

The 1960s' and 1970s' population censuses do not yield high-resolution data to map such differences, but a number of surveys and squatter studies and an excellent monograph by Tuğrul Akçura provide empirical evidence on the contrast between the social profiles of formal and informal sectors.[9] Those with white-collar occupations formed enclaves in southern Ankara (Güvenevleri, Kavaklıdere, and Çankaya). In 1970, white-collar occupations accounted for no less than 65 percent of the active population in these prestigious neighborhoods, whereas the city average was on the order of 9 percent.[10] A sharper contrast is reported for those with advanced education, with densities as low as 3 percent in squatter settlements. This sharp social polarization triggered an internal differentiation of central business district functions. The historical city center nearer to squatter settlements specialized in trades and activities attractive to low-income groups, and the new city specialized in retailing and services oriented to the well-to-do who resided in southern sectors. The internal differentiation affected employment profiles: southerners were overrepresented in the southern part and northerners in the northern sectors of the central business district.[11]

THE SOCIAL GEOGRAPHY OF ANKARA IN THE 1990S

The publication of data from the 1990 census was a turning point for urban studies in Turkey. This information was particularly useful in drawing maps based on major variables such as schooling, economic activity, province of origin, housing tenure, and household size. Even a casual observer could detect the boundary separating the well-educated, well-to-do south and southwestern sectors from the deprived north and northeast; the donut-shaped contiguous compact city is no longer there. The transformations reflect the impact of intra-urban mobility, demography, and labor market characteristics, and serve as a proxy measure of social deprivation, cultural capital, and social distinction.

The 1990s were turbulent years in Turkey's social history. Studies of housing, economic activity, birthplace, housing tenure, education, and household size show that apart from southern and northwesterns quadrants, few areas emerge with high social and welfare indicators (i.e., smaller household sizes, concentration of high-ranking executives born in western provinces, overrepresentation of those in producer and social services and in scientific technical professions, public executives, etc.).[12] The northeastern and southeastern quadrants show distinctly different profiles (i.e., blue collar, eastern born, etc.). We start to see that intra-urban mobility does not alleviate but helps to consolidate these differences. The intra-urban household mobility transformed 1970s north-south social contrast into a contrast between the inner and outer sectors of Ankara.

CONCLUSION

Ankara's growth was associated with significant morphological changes and transformation in its urban fabric. The latter is closely linked with the three distinct phases of Turkey's urbanization as well as with local contingencies. During the first decades of the Republican era, Ankara grew from a small provincial town into the second-largest city of the newly established nation-state. The transition to a multiparty system put an end to its de facto most-favored-city status. Yet despite inhospitable economic and political conditions, major actors and stakeholders in land use and planning were fairly active. They devised innovative measures to address traffic congestion, environmental degradation, mass housing, proactive planning, red tape, and development land acquisition. Endowed with limited planning power and funds, municipalities were able to improve public services and steer and implement plans via strategic development land supply. The transition from containment to decentralization observed in the third phase of the city's development was not left to the vagaries of the land market but was to a large extent prepared in advance. The new city form, though decentralized, cannot be considered a case of urban sprawl; the form is organized in an inherently different way. Net densities do not decrease significantly with distance to the central business district, as was the case in the early 1980s.

Between 1990 and 2000, Ankara deepened its specialization in the service sector while Istanbul and Izmir, gateways more exposed to global flows, experienced different structural transformations and a faster pace of development. The capital-city status enabled Ankara to preserve its distinctive features; it is now a center of excellence in health, higher education, and new technologies and has important electronics and software engineering industries.

Squatter neighborhoods in Ankara, 2005.

CHALLENGES AHEAD

Turkey is about to complete its demographic and urban transition process. The latest nationwide demographic and health surveys show fertility rates at lower than replacement level. In this context, urban growth depends entirely on net migration. A demographic simulation experiment for Istanbul shows that should migration stop, population would gradually stabilize, than decline. The same surely holds true for Ankara. Meanwhile, negotiations with the European Union and the adoption of structural adjustment programs of the International Monetary Fund have hastened rationalization in Turkey's agriculture. These processes will ultimately affect the distribution of population and capital.

In the last twenty years, the relaxation of urban containment policies, increasing investments in urban thoroughfares and in mass transit systems, increased car ownership, and the completion of major mass housing projects enhanced intra-urban mobility, while the proliferation of shopping malls gave added impetus to the transition from the compact city of the 1970s to a new decentralized urban macro form. The urban fabric of Ankara in the mid-1990s was inherently different than that of the 1970s and had few common features with 1950s' Ankara. Southern sectors of the inner city were intensely affected by these changes as a consequence of rising land prices, and squatter settlements are experiencing a swift process of gentrification. Pictures taken in 2005 from squatter neighborhoods in the southwestern quadrant depict the magnitude of land use transformations. It follows that the "forgotten, and forsaken" village of Balgat, described as "a colorless, shapeless dump," is no longer there. Today it constitutes one of the many major subcenters of the city, which includes the ministry of foreign affairs, the national headquarters of three major political parties, major shopping malls, and private hospitals and universities, with subway and intercity bus terminals.

This overview on the urban history of Ankara shows that the production of urban space and adaptation to new contexts are not insurmountable obstacles. But we have also seen that the considerable successes in producing new spaces did not alleviate but led to the redefinition of segregation, exclusion, enclaves, and the emergence of disconnected subcultures. As is elsewhere the case, opposition between the traditional and the modern, the formal and the informal—reflected in the variant social profiles of the inner city and the metropolitan fringes—constitutes perhaps the major urban problem of Ankara.

Notes

1. This critical realist approach to urban historiography is explained in many articles and books by Ilhan Tekeli; for the latest and one of the most concise expositions, see Tekeli, "A New Paradigm Proposal for Urban Historiography," in *Republic's Ankara*, T. Enyapılı, ed. (Ankara: Middle East Technical University Press, 2005), pp. 3–21.

2. Ilhan Tekeli et al., *City of Squatters, Shared Taxis, and Street Vendors* (Istanbul: Cem, 1976) (in Turkish).

3. The latter figure extracted from the 1980 census taken right after the coup d'état is most probably an undercount. But even using a low figure, the population tripled within twenty years.

4. Daniel Lerner, "The Grocer and the Chief: A Parable," in *Urbanism in World Perspective*, Sylvia F. Fava, ed. (New York: T.Y. Crowell Company, 1963), p. 370.

5. Peter Hall et al., *The Containment of Urban England* (London: Allen and Unwin, 1973).

6. See John R. Clark, "Comparison of the Population Density Gradients of the Planned and Unplanned Sections of Ankara," *Population and Migration Trends in Eastern Europe* (Boulder, CO: Westview Press, 1977), pp. 135–156.

7. Positive and negative aspects of the contained city macro form are discussed in *The 2015 Structural Plan Report*. See Ilhan Tekeli et al., *Ankara from 1985 to 2015: English Summary* (Ankara: Greater Ankara Municipality, 1968), p. 180.

8. CAMP-Harris Mesera, *Ankara Project: Water Supply*, Vol. 1 (Ankara: 1969).

9. Tuğrul Akçura, *Ankara: A Monograph on the Capital of the Republic of Turkey* (Ankara: Middle East Technical University Press, 1971) (in Turkish).

10. Ibid., p. 547.

11. Ibid.

12. This is an empirical result derived from a concatenated analysis of Turkey's employment figures from 1990 and 2000 by economic sectors of activity and provinces. For simple examples, see Michael Greenacre, "Correspondence Analysis and Its Interpretation," in *Correspondence Analysis in the Social Sciences*, Michael Greenacre and J. Blasius, eds. (London: Academic Press, 1994), pp. 3–22.

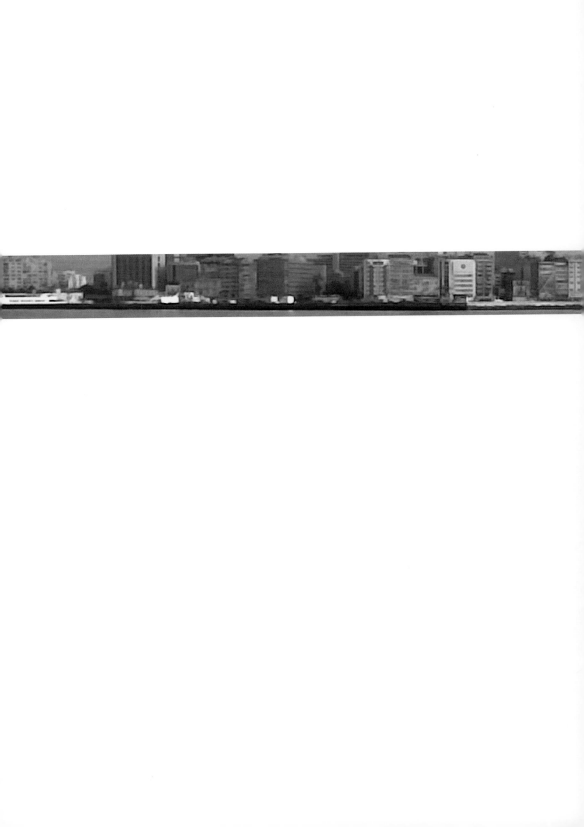

CEMAL ARKON

IZMIR

IN THE REPUBLICAN PERIOD

In 1923 began a series of developments that were important for today's urban silhouette of Izmir. These developments signaled the birth of a new state as well as the reconstruction of a country devastated by war. Izmir was the second-largest city in Turkey in 1923, and today it is the third-largest, the second-largest port, and an industrial and tourism center of the country. This chapter is a summary of urban planning studies and spatial developments in Izmir in the period since the Republic was formed. It has two parts. After a short introduction to Izmir, the first part focuses on urban planning studies done during the Republican period, and urban restructuring and transformation processes set in motion after the 1980s. The second part includes a general evaluation of the urbanization process of the recent past and some recommendations for future planning.

INTRODUCTION

The bay of Izmir is one of the largest on the Aegean coast of Turkey. This geographic characteristic made the city a hub for trade with Europe and allowed it to play an important regional economic role as an export center for Turkey's agricultural hinterland. The historic development of Izmir intersects with its geographic location to establish its strategic position today; over time, its national, regional, and international importance has risen dramatically.

The location of Izmir also gave it the opportunity to develop trade and industrial activities in the city, and a transformation began to appear in the spatial structure of Izmir starting from the second part of the nineteenth century. In this period the population of the city was around 200,000, and a large part consisted of ethnic and religious minorities (Armenians, Jews, etc.). Differentiation in income was reflected on the spatial organization of the city more clearly at the end of this century. While upper-income groups and non-Muslim populations settled in the vicinity of the center, middle- and low-income groups lived in the areas around the Kadifekale district.

In the first half of the twentieth century, and in the first years of the Republic, national development policies were based on the industrialization of the country. In 1927, Izmir was the second-largest city (the first was Istanbul) in terms of industrial establishments. Today it accounts for 7.4 percent of industrial production and is the second-largest port, with 18 percent of exports and 13 percent of imports. Izmir experienced rapid urbanization after the 1950s, when migration started from rural areas to the towns and cities. Today, within the new metropolitan municipality boundary, the estimated population is around 3,400,000.

Izmir
+

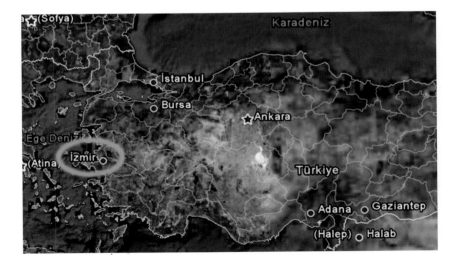

PLANNING STUDIES SINCE 1923

In the new Turkish Republic, one of the primary problems facing the Izmir city government was significant damage to the city center caused by a great fire, which decimated almost all of the center, leaving only the periphery of the old city intact. It is estimated that the fire destroyed 20,000–25,000 buildings, or three-fourths of the city center. In spite of the great devastation and drop in population from 350,000 to 180,000 and the accompanying decrease in commercial activities, Izmir was still the second-largest city in the country. Yet the cultural and social topography of the city had changed. The fire had mostly affected minority neighborhoods; afterward, there was a great migration of foreigners and minorities and a decrease in trade activities (Serçe, Yilmaz, and Yetkin 2003).

Prost-Danger Plan: The fire, however, had opened the way for the construction of a modern city center with the help of a new master plan (Serçe, Yilmaz, and Yetkin 2003). The first master plan of Izmir was developed by the French planner Rene Danger. Rene and Raymond Danger were brothers working under the supervision of Henri Prost; thus this plan is known as the "Prost-Danger Plan." The plan was completed and submitted to the Izmir municipality in 1925. It was primarily a zoning plan and mostly covered burned-out parts of the central area. The only construction project undertaken according to the Prost-Danger Plan, aside from modifications of a few roads, was Cumhuriyet Square.

Boundaries of the Greater City of Izmir Municipality, approved by Law 5216 in 2004 (GIM archives).

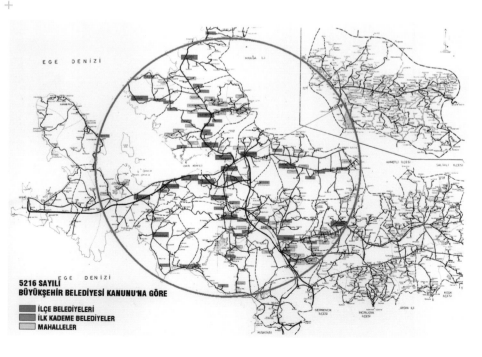

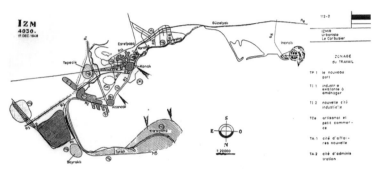

Top: Danger-Prost plan's treatment of a fire zone, after being modified by the municipal technical committee (GIM archives).

MIddle: Le Corbusier's plan (GIM archives).

Bottom: K. Ahmet Aru, Emin Canpolat, and Gündüz Özde master plan, 1952 (GIM archives).

Le Corbusier Plan: In 1930, Karşıyaka, Bayraklı, Turan, and in 1937 Inciraltı were included within the municipal boundaries, extending the city over an area of about 5,800 hectares, with a population of approximately 190,000. By 1945, this population had increased by only 10,000. In 1939, for the preparation of a new master plan, the Izmir municipality had established contact with Le Corbusier. But World War II had started, and Le Corbusier would not come to Izmir until the summer of 1948. His plan was designed around the idea of a "green city" and proposed 1,000 acres of new green space; the plan also reserved the area between Bayraklı and Alsancak and some parts of Bornova for future industrial developments. Le Corbusier, predicting a city population of 400,000 for the year 2000, proposed to transform the historical structure of the city. This master plan had no chance to be implemented, however, and was shelved in the municipality archives.

Aru, Canpolat, Özde Plan: In 1950, the population of Izmir municipality was around 250,000. In 1951, the municipality sponsored an international master plan competition. The winner was a plan prepared by Kemal Ahmet Aru that proposed the axis of Güzelyalı toward Inciraltı for recreation and sports facilities, and Halkapinar and Bayrakli for industrial and commercial uses. Karşıyaka was planned as a semicircle, including Turan, Soğukkuyu, and Bostanlı, with the port at the center (Serçe, Yılmaz, and Yetkin 2003). This plan was approved in 1955, but subsequent revisions changed it dramatically. The most important reason for the failure of Aru's plan was the underestimation of population growth.

Albert Bodmer Plan: From 1950 to 1960, the population of Izmir doubled, to 500,000. This increase created serious problems for the city. Half of this growth was realized within the municipal boundaries, and the rest was adjacent. The incoming population in this period was settled without planning control. The Bodmer Plan was prepared in 1960, but not officially approved. It was mainly a revision plan. This plan predicted the city's population to be 900,000 by 2000. In the plan, the road system was improved, a new peripheral road connected northern and southern parts of the city, and new connections for a heavy-industry zone on the east axis of the city were proposed. This plan focused on the area within the boundaries of the municipality, though Bodmer acknowledged that its success would depend on addressing the adjacent settlements as well.

Metropolitan Master Plan: After the 1960s, a rapid outward movement took place, resulting in the extensive linear expansion of urban development along the major transportation axes extending north (Karşıyaka), east (Bornova), and south (Güzelbahçe). Today all the settlements around Izmir Bay are connected, forming an urban ring that extends outward approximately 30 kilometers from the city core of the Konak district.

In 1968, the Metropolitan Planning Bureau of Izmir was established to prepare a master plan of Izmir. This plan, covering all of the metropolitan region and the municipalities in 1972, was approved in 1973. The metropolitan master plan covered the municipalities of Central Izmir, Büyük Çiğli, Bornova, Pınarbaşı, Çamdibi, Altındağ, Gültepe, Buca, Gaziemir, Yeşilyurt, Balçova, Narlıdere, and Güzelbahçe. This plan stimulated the landuse pattern in which new industrial areas were proposed to relocate pollutant industry; new residential areas were planned close to major industrial zones; maximum densities were determined for industrial and residential zones; historical heritage and natural assets were protected against deterioration; and lands required for social and technical infrastructure were reserved for future developments.

The plan proposed two main industrial zones: the Şemikler-Çiğli-Menemen district to the north and the Karabağlar-Gaziemir-Cumaovas to the south. A linear city macro form was proposed along the north-south axis. Small manufacturing enterprises and warehouses located in the inner city were moved to the new development axis. On this axis, warehousing zones were planned to be close to the harbor and to railway and highway connections (Arkon and Gülerman 1995). *Gecekondu* (squatter housing) areas were proposed for redevelopment.

The population predicted by the metropolitan master plan was 1,466,000 for 1985 (close to the actual population of 1,489,000 in that year). Since 1973, the metropolitan master plan has been revised several times, devolving into the current collection of partial amendments. This failure could be attributed to a number of causes, including the fact that the master plan was not able to keep pace with the dynamic processes observed during the period, and the chronic lack of resources available for plan implementation. During the plan period, illegal housing developments expanded into areas

Master plan revision, 1989 (GIM archives).

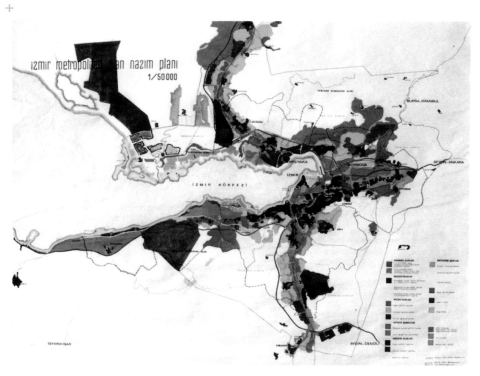

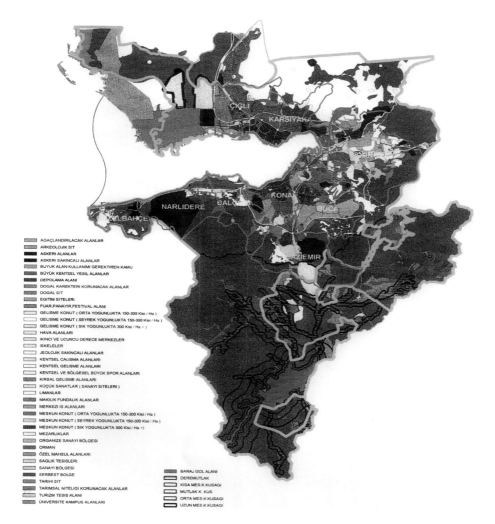

Main investment areas in the outer parts of the city (Kompil 2005).

that should have been reserved for other purposes, especially social and technical infrastructure.

Urban Restructuring and Transformation Processes after the 1980s: The year 1984 was a milestone in the history of metropolitan government in Turkey. The Law of Greater City Municipalities gave a special "greater city/metropolis" status to Izmir. A two-tiered system, with metropolitan and district municipalities, was introduced in the metropolitan areas. According to this law, metropolitan municipalities have the duty to prepare, approve, and implement master plans, and district municipalities are in charge of preparing zoning (implementation) plans, which have to be consistent with the master plan of the greater city (metropolitan) municipalities (Kok 2004).

Izmir was confronted with the urban restructuring process that ran parallel to the neoliberal transformations in the country. Changes in the economy and politics starting from early 1980s strongly influenced the social, institutional, and spatial structures in urban areas. In 2004, a new Law of Greater City Municipalities was approved, and the boundaries of Izmir were extended 50 kilometers in all directions.

Many large-scale projects have changed the urban landscape of Izmir (Kok 2004). These fragmented developments spread out across the city in an uncoordinated way. Also in this period, the objective of planning changed from comprehensive to incremental approaches, promoting individual projects. The most striking example of the incremental planning approach in Izmir was the international urban design competition for the Alsancak-Turan district, announced in 2001. The competition area covered almost 600 hectares, without the support of a master plan. A particular type of spatial project became common: scattered large-scale partial projects in certain parts of the city— along the major transportation axes or combining different land uses as part of the development or redevelopment of a large area. With these types of developments, Izmir experienced urban sprawl in almost all directions. Turkey, at the periphery of advanced capitalist urban dynamics, is increasingly shaped by the globalization of property markets. This reality gives the private sector negotiating power (as the public sector is constantly in need of additional capital), which it uses to define the location, function, and condition of projects (Kok 2004). In 1989, the Greater Izmir Municipality prepared and approved a revision of the 1/25,000-scale master plan, which is made up by combining zoning plans at 1/1,000-scale prepared by the district municipalities. But in 2003, this revision plan was cancelled by the Council of State, based on the argument that approval authority of 1/25,000-scale plans belongs to the Ministry of Public Works and Urban Development. Following the decision of the Council of State, the Ministry of Public Works and Urban Development cancelled the 1973 master plan, arguing that this plan no longer addressed current needs. Since then, there has been no greater city master plan of Izmir in force.

Since 2000, the greater municipality of Izmir has been in the process of restructuring its public transportation network and services. One of these upgrades is the integration of light-rail transit (LRT), ferries, and bus systems. Another restructuring in transportation is the upgrading of commuter train lines operated by the Turkish state railways between Aliağa and Cumaovası and its integration with the LRT system.

EVALUATION OF THE URBANIZATION PROCESS OF IZMIR IN THE REPUBLICAN PERIOD

Given growing settlement concentrations, almost all coastal sections of the Greater Izmir Municipality (GIM) have been under strong pressure in terms of physical occupation of space. If this trend continues, reflecting population pressure and extensive utilization of land for urban purposes, it is possible to expect that Izmir will double its urban area over the next twenty to twenty-five years. The presence of numerous municipalities in GIM; the absence of sufficient technical infrastructure and experience; and the lack of large-scale subregional planning and means of implementation and supervision result in a problematic sprawl of second homes and tourist establishments that threaten the natural assets of the coastline. The establishment of subregional planning units and the development of an administrative database would help to ease these problems.

Continuing migration and illegal property development are still troubling issues for Izmir. The lack of effective planning measures, underdeveloped social housing policy, and inadequate private investment in the housing sector are the major housing problems. Although it is expected that the population growth of Turkey will stabilize around 2050 at 90–100 million, until then, migration from rural to urban areas will continue due to the inequity among regions of the country as well as modifications in agricultural policies arising from globalization and integration with the European Union. Given its location, the fertility of the agricultural areas in its hinterland, and its climate, Izmir will continue to be one of the prime metropolitan areas to receive migration. The incoming population will be mostly uneducated and will seek work as unskilled labor.

Recent migrants to Izmir and lower-income urban residents had attempted to meet their housing needs with squatter houses. Housing areas around the urban center have thus depreciated and become the residential space of lower-income groups. The emergence of new *gecekondu* areas constructed after laws legalized these developments has tended to undermine urban development and planning. The spread of such developments raises a number of social and technical infrastructure and environmental issues. These include whether and how services such as water, sewerage, electricity, and transportation should be supplied to such developments and how to deal with wastewater discharges.

Possible solutions to these problems would include: formulating radical policies (i.e., effective social and cultural investment programs) to overcome the development gap among regions, which would serve as countermigration incentives, assisting lower-income urban populations in building their own houses; and developing inexpensive long-term housing loan programs.

Urban sprawl arising from the development of the middle-income group's mass housing and the upper-income group's "villa-type" housing threatens agricultural land and forest areas. Large tracts of farmland with high economic value (for example, olive groves on the coastal area between Dikili and Aliağa districts, in Urla; farmland in the Kemalpaşa plain; citrus fruit areas in Narlıdere, Gümüldür, and Balçova, etc.) are destroyed by urban developments. Inadequate regulation and local enforcement have also permitted developments on historic and natural sites. The low-quality urban environment, lacking social and technical infrastructure, is evident in middle-income housing areas comprised mainly of multistory detached apartment buildings sprawling on the fringe, particularly along the northern axis of Izmir. The demands of upper-income groups for "gated communities" on the urban fringe, particularly in the 1990s, was met in ways that both damaged the natural environment and underscored socioeconomic segregation: such housing areas are sprawling rapidly, especially along the western axis of Izmir, on forest land and predominantly at the cost of olive groves.

To overcome of the negative effects of urban sprawl, the following proposals could be developed: the adoption of policies (taxation, conservation, development supervision, etc.) that encourage development on the urban fringe to evolve in tandem with infrastructural investments; the establishment of a planning unit to produce up-to-date information and facilitate communication among local administrative bodies, investors, local people, and nongovernmental organizations; the production of strategic plans and implementation policies to meet the demands for housing; and the allocation of investments within the entirety of the metropolitan area.

Environmental pollution from unplanned and uncontrolled urban developments and the byproducts of agricultural production has fouled vital river basins (Büyük Menderes, Küçük Menderes, Gediz, and Tahtalı). The results of this misuse are water and soil pollution, low water table levels, and poor quality and quantity in agricultural production. Industrial activities at Nemrut and Aliağa Bays, West of Büyük Çişli, and developments of second homes along the coastal strip are the major threats to the conservation of the natural coastal assets of the GIM region. The inability to preserve wetlands near the metropolitan area is another planning problem. Several actions could address environmental pollution: coordination in governance, planning, and investment; determination of priority problem areas and production of attendant policies, investments, and preservation decisions; and constitution of an administrative plan for special sites such as wetlands.

Although the metropolitan area is in a major earthquake zone, local building construction is not directed at reducing risks—another serious problem in Izmir. Continued building on filled ground, on sites with high groundwater levels, and on other inappropriate sites carries the potential of great human and material loss in the event of an earthquake. The following precautions could reduce such risks: conducting geological and geotechnical analyses in current and potential metropolitan development areas; conducting micro-zoning studies; reanalyzing new development according to the results obtained in these studies; undertaking improvement/demolition where necessary; and establishing stronger supervisory mechanisms for future development.

Squatter developments and illegal buildings have sprung up in recent years within the city, even in central areas. Urban regeneration projects are being developed in relation to these developments. The new urban environments constituted by regeneration projects, however, at times introduce serious problems and at others actually decrease the well-being of established residents. Extensive "improvement plans" were approved during 1985–1999. Some of these plans that featured the demolition and redevelopment of both squatter housing and other illegal buildings were problematic (such as in the case of the Narlıdere-Narkent development). Urban regeneration projects must be based on detailed analysis, include user participation, and not be driven by market conditions alone.

CONCLUSION

The lack of a unified planning institution for the entire metropolitan area that would foster continuous, dynamic, and participatory processes is a major problem in the urbanization of Izmir. The decentralization of municipal government leads to fragmented decision making. Communication among the various layers of government does not happen efficiently.

A strategic plan enabling decision making for macro investments in transportation, energy, industry, conservation of the natural environment, and the development of policies concerning all major settlement regions has not been prepared for the past two decades. The result has been fragmentary investment decisions that frequently are at odds, waste resources, and do substantial damage to both urban and natural environments.

An "Izmir Metropolitan Area Planning Unit" should be established to encompass all major settlements of the metropolitan whole. Using a participatory working process and including specialists from a variety of disciplines, this unit ought to produce a strategic plan for the entire metropolitan region. Micro-level plans can then be made coherent with the macro decisions taken in the framework of the strategic plan.

References

Arkon, C., and A. R. Gülerman. 1995. "Izmir Büyükşehir Bütünündeki Nazım Plan Çalışmaları Üzerine Bir İnceleme." *Planlama* 95/1–2. Ankara.

Kok, T. T. 2004. "Budapest, Istanbul, and Warsaw—Institutional and Spatial Change." Netherlands: Eburon Academic Publishers.

Kompil, E. 2005. "Uneven Development and Declining Inner-City Residential Areas: The Case of Izmir–Tuzcu District." Unpublished dissertation, I.I.T. Izmir.

Priority Actions Program—Regional Activity Center. 1992. Mediterranean Action Plan Interim Report. Split.

Serçe, E., F. Yılmaz, and S. Yetkin. 2003. "The City That Rose from the Ashes." Kent Kitaplığı Dizisi: 45, Izmir.

CONTRIBUTORS

ILHAN TEKELI received a Bachelor of Arts in Civil Engineering from Istanbul Technical University (1960), a Master of Science in City and Regional Planning from Middle East Technical University (1966), and a Ph.D. in City Planning from ITU (1968). He has taught in the City and Regional Planning Department of Middle East Technical University since 1970. Tekeli is the author of more than 50 books and 400 articles in the areas of city and regional planning, planning theory, micro-geography, geography of migration and political behavior, theory and history of local administration in Turkey, urbanizations and urban policy, economic policy, economic history of Turkey, and the history of cities and society. He is the author of *Türkiye'de Belediyeciliğin Evrimi* (1978), *The Development of the İstanbul Metropolitan Area: Urban Administration and Planning* (1994), and *Mimar Kemalettin'in Yazdıkları* (1997). Tekeli has won several social science awards and has been a member of the consultancy committees of many municipalities and organizations. He is founder of the Economic and Social History Foundation of Turkey and of the Executive Committee of the World Academy for Local Government and Democracy.

MURAT GUVENÇ is a professor of city and regional planning at Bilgi University in Istanbul. Prior to that, he taught at Middle East Technical University in Ankara, where he also served as consultant for the city's master planning efforts. He is author of several publications on Turkish urbanism, urban poverty, mapping, and demographic changes in cities. He is currently completing an urban atlas of Istanbul.

ZEYNEP MEREY ENLIL is an associate professor at the Yıldız Technical University, Faculty of Architecture, Department of City and Regional Planning. Enlil is the leader of the research team of the Cultural Industries and Tourism Unit at the Istanbul Metropolitan Planning and Urban Design Center.

HÜSEYIN KAPTAN is a professor at the Yıldız Technical University, Faculty of Architecture, Department of City and Regional Planning, in Istanbul. From 2005 to 2008, he directed the Istanbul Metropolitan Planning and Urban Design Center.

CEMAL ARKON is a professor at the Izmir Institute of Technology, Department of City and Regional Planning.